DODGERS
TO
DAMASCUS

DODGERS
TO
DAMASCUS

David Lesch's Journey
from Baseball to the Middle East

CATHERINE NIXON COOKE

Foreword by Peter C. Goldmark

TRINITY UNIVERSITY PRESS
SAN ANTONIO, TEXAS

Trinity University Press
San Antonio, Texas 78212

Copyright © 2025 by Catherine Nixon Cooke

Foreword copyright © 2025 by Peter C. Goldmark

All rights reserved. No part of this book may be reproduced in any form or by any electronic or mechanical means, including information storage and retrieval systems, without permission in writing from the publisher.

Book design by BookMatters, Berkeley
Jacket design by Crystal Hollis / Seale Studios
Jacket images, collection of David Lesch
Author photo by Robert Maxham

ISBN 978-1-59534-323-9 hardcover
ISBN 978-1-59534-324-6 ebook

Trinity University Press strives to produce its books using methods and materials in an environmentally sensitive manner. We favor working with manufacturers that practice sustainable management of all natural resources, produce paper using recycled stock, and manage forests with the best possible practices for people, biodiversity, and sustainability. The press is a member of the Green Press Initiative, a nonprofit program dedicated to supporting publishers in their efforts to reduce their impacts on endangered forests, climate change, and forest-dependent communities.

The paper used in this publication meets the minimum requirements of the American National Standard for Information Sciences—Permanence of Paper for Printed Library Materials, ansi 39.48–1992.

CIP data on file at the Library of Congress

29 28 27 26 25 | 5 4 3 2 1

For the peacemakers of the world

who know the importance of listening

to diverse voices with open minds and hearts

CONTENTS

Foreword, by Peter C. Goldmark   ix

A Dangerous Drink   1

The Road to Dodgertown   9

Welcome to Mars   23

Curveballs   37

Finding Home Base   59

Horizons of History   89

In the Lion's Den   115

The Path of Abraham   135

Death and Diplomacy   159

Pioneering the Possible   185

Syrian Surprise   215

Epilogue   229

Acknowledgments   245
Image Credits   249
Bibliography   251
Index   257

FOREWORD

PETER C. GOLDMARK

Do you feel lost some of the time? Almost all of us do in this fluid period of impetuous polarization, unreliable information, and declining trust in our public institutions, including our government and the free press.

I suggest that you take a journey with David Lesch. In *Dodgers to Damascus*, Catherine Nixon Cooke invites readers to join Lesch as he bursts forward to athletic prominence in his teens, learning to handle demanding physical performance, public attention and flattery, and the need for enormous internal concentration and psychological focus for his ambition. When he falls victim to an injury that closes one of the most promising baseball careers of his generation, Lesch reinvents himself. Cooke takes readers on the new arc of his incredible life journey to become a teacher, confidante, trusted intermediary, profound listener, practical constructor of possibilities, and a respected guide to the cradle of civilization, a region marked by religious conflict, complex governments, and a history of volatility—the Middle East.

Dodgers to Damascus is the powerful story of the life of an amazing American. After you have read it, set aside some quiet time to reflect on what you can learn from this wonderful biography as you prepare to navigate one of the most challenging and dangerous periods in our history on the only planet we will ever have.

A Sufi dancer performs at a dinner honoring the Lesch family, Syria, 2008

A DANGEROUS DRINK

SYRIA, 2008

Dusk crept across the Arabian Desert in shades of mauve and faint tangerine. Just a few miles south of the oldest continuously inhabited city on earth, an official black sedan sped toward an ancient stone villa where twinkling party lights and Sufi musicians in the courtyard welcomed arriving guests. But David Lesch could not savor the soft colors of the sky or the beauty of the destination just ahead. He could barely see them. His vision blurred; his head throbbed; he felt a strange tingling in his legs and a weakness that frightened him. He grabbed Judy Dunlap's hand and mumbled that he was unsure if he could exit the automobile.

Judy was reassuring, reminding David of preparations for a spectacular farewell party to honor him on their last night in Syria. Syria—the word conjured paradoxical images as David struggled with growing brain fog. Syria—one of the most complicated countries in the world, described by author Mark Twain in 1869 as the fabled Garden of Eden, the home of exotic princes and genii of *The Arabian Nights*. Syria—where more than 13 million citizens have been displaced, 7 million have fled the country, and more than 600,000 have died since its civil war began in 2011. As he held Judy's hand, David feared he might be destined to join those lost souls.

He had been poisoned before and knew the symptoms, could even pinpoint the moment earlier in the day when the security official assigned to take the Lesch family to ancient Palmyra had offered him a special drink. He had felt no dizziness on that perfect morning, sipping sweet tea from a thermos offered by the government agent and exploring the ancient desert oasis halfway between the Mediterranean Sea and the Euphrates River. A major route of east-west trade in the third century BCE, now a UNESCO World Heritage Site, it once connected the Roman world with Mesopotamia. David had told Judy and his eighteen-year-old son, Michael, the history of its monuments and temples, thousands of years old, unaware that the extremist group Islamic State in Iraq and the Levant would later demolish many of them in 2015, including the pagan Temple of Baal. But on that beautiful sunny day in 2008 David did not anticipate the looming tragedy nor the personal loss it would bring. Their guide at Palmyra was a dear friend, Dr. Khalid al-Asaad, the head of antiquities for the site. He would be one of the victims of the future attack, beheaded at the age of eighty-two by ISIS.

By midday a queasiness alerted him that the special drink was questionable, and the feeling was all too familiar. The year before, while on a special mission in Syria, he had been poisoned and lay bedridden in Damascus. *Why poison me?*, David had wondered then. As a Western author working on an authorized biography of Syria's president Bashar al-Assad, he had been warmly welcomed in 2004. He met often with the country's young president, who was tall and smiling, always dressed in a blue blazer. Together they discussed al-Assad's medical studies in England, and the family tragedy that ended his dream of becoming an eye surgeon, prompting his return to Syria in 1994 to become his father's heir apparent. When Hafez al-Assad died in 2000, after thirty years of rule, Bashar al-Assad stepped into a much different future. In December of that year, he had married Asma Fawaz Akhras, a beautiful and stylish twenty-five-year-old raised in London and formerly employed by J.P. Morgan in New York. She presented a fresh vision of modernity to an ancient land, and he carried the potential for cultural and political transformation.

David's resulting book, *The New Lion of Damascus: Bashar al-Asad and Modern Syria* (2005), reflected the world's hope that Bashar al-Assad would become a much-needed reformer in his country. *Assad* (*Asad*) means "lion" in English. His late father Hafez liked the translation and had certainly lived up to it during his long, stern rule. The international community watched now as his cub stepped into power, wondering if the twenty-first century might bring a gentler ruling style to Syria. But over the next few years, it became clear that early hopes for change were not likely to happen. Bashar appeared to be adopting his father's approach to leadership.

As familiar waves of nausea swept over him now, David wondered if he would survive and, if he did, whether he would be allowed back into the country. He questioned the wisdom of returning to this complex country, where mounting turmoil was palpable in Damascus and the desert towns far beyond the capital. Had he misjudged the cordial invitation from Syrian friends to show Judy and Michael the wonders of the ancient sites he knew so well? With a doctorate in Middle Eastern history from Harvard University, he had conducted research and published multiple books about that part of the world. He was a well-known professor at Trinity University in San Antonio, Texas, and many Syrian academics, diplomats, and businessmen had befriended him over the years.

His extensive knowledge, access to Syrian leadership, and frequent trips to the Middle East had resulted in special assignments from US government agencies, the United Nations, and NGOs. In fact, the 2008 trip was more than just a family adventure. He was on a special mission, the brainchild of Harvard's Program on Negotiation in cooperation with the Carter Center—not classified but a bit under the radar. While the journey was an opportunity to share firsthand the history and culture of a place he had described for so long to Judy and Michael, David was also pursuing an innovative international idea for resolving the conflicts that had plagued the region for centuries. Now he wondered if a darker force was at work in the group of Syrian business leaders and diplomats he had come to trust.

As he grappled with doubts and dizziness, a dreamlike vision floated through his mind. He was standing on the pitcher's mound at Dodger Stadium, cheers from the stands echoing down to the field. He felt a surge of adrenaline as he looked toward home plate. He had worked hard to reach this pinnacle in baseball, as the Los Angeles Dodgers' number one draft pick in 1980 and as the pride of Bel Air, Maryland. He was nineteen years old when the country's most respected MLB team recruited him. He planned to follow in the famous footsteps of one of his idols, Sandy Koufax, whose ninety-five-mile-an-hour fastball struck fear in every batter. Focus. Assess everything happening on the diamond. Step onto the mound's rubber plate. Begin the wind-up. Take a breath.

Judy's voice pulled him back, catapulting him forward through the decades, from the imagined sun-drenched vista of Los Angeles back to the outskirts of Damascus. He focused on the bright lights of the villa in the distance, tried to assess the situation, and wondered again if this adventure would end badly for him and his family.

David had visited Syria more than thirty times, living there for months on some occasions. He had written his dissertation on its history. He clearly understood that its modern perceptions are not the full picture, noting that today's Syria is a country known for all the wrong reasons: civil war, vicious sectarianism, rampant death and destruction, a massive refugee exodus, and terrorism. He had seen firsthand that there was much more beneath that dark surface.

While the modern nation of Syria is about the size of North Dakota, measuring 71,504 square miles, many Syrians consider the arbitrary boundaries created by the Europeans after World War I to represent just a portion of Bilad al-Sham, or Greater Syria. Present-day Lebanon, Jordan, Israel, and parts of Turkey are included in the larger whole, known in the West as the Levant. This fertile crescent was named by ancient traders, and the term *levant* translates from its Italian root as "rising" or "east," referring to the direction where the sun rises, used to describe the eastern Mediterranean region.

Perfectly positioned on the oldest known trade route, it is a true crossroads of history. Different empires and peoples have traversed this territory for millennia, creating a cultural mosaic enriched by the intermingling of belief systems, government structures, and ethnic traditions. It is home to some of the world's most magnificent historical and archeological landmarks. Palmyra (Tadmur), founded in the third century BCE, is an oasis in the desert that became an important Roman trade way station on the East-West caravan route, along with Petra in Jordan. The Krak des Chevaliers is the best-preserved Crusader castle in the Middle East, where the Knights Hospitaller protected the Christian Crusader presence in the Holy Land during the twelfth century. Syria's ancient capital, Damascus, is home to the "Street Called Straight," where Saint Paul is said to have experienced his conversion to Christianity. Not far away, nestled in the mountains, the largely Christian town of Maaloula is known as the last place on earth where Aramaic, the language of Jesus of Nazareth, is still spoken.

The rest of the country is full of historical and religious sites belonging to Syria's dominant religion, Islam, which became a major presence within two years after the death of the Prophet Muhammad in the seventh century. Before he began his religious calling in 610 CE from his home in Mecca, Muhammad traveled the deserts and hills in trade caravans throughout western Arabia (the Hijaz) and most likely northward through the Holy Land and to Damascus. The progenitor of a new religion that revered Old and New Testament prophets such as Abraham, Moses, and Jesus, he was following in his ancestors' footsteps as he traversed the Middle East. Centuries before, Abraham (Ibrahim), revered as the "Father Prophet" by Jews, Christians, and Muslims around the world, had made a similar journey.

According to religious scriptures from all three faiths, sometime around 1900 BCE the Lord told Abraham to leave his home and country to deliver an important message in a new land that He would show him. Moses left Ur, near the mouth of the Euphrates in ancient Mesopotamia, and traveled through the Middle East to deliver his message of the existence of one God, urging his people to renounce the worship of idols. His pilgrimage took him through what is now Iraq, Egypt, Saudi Arabia, Syria, Jordan, Lebanon, Israel, and finally Palestine, where he died around 1815 BCE at the ripe old age of 175. He was buried in the Cave of the Patriarchs near Hebron, a holy city for followers of Islam, Judaism, and Christianity. It is ironic that today his tomb, shared by a mosque and a synagogue, is in one of the Middle East's most conflicted cities.

The Prophet Abraham was partly responsible for David Lesch's work in Syria from 2007 through 2009. So were some high-level US government officials, who were watching the growing turmoil

Michael Lesch, David Lesch, and Judy Dunlap in Syria, 2008

in Syria with dismay and knew he was a man well suited for a unique role in the developing international drama. Not fazed by the challenges, David attributed his ability to overcome them to baseball.

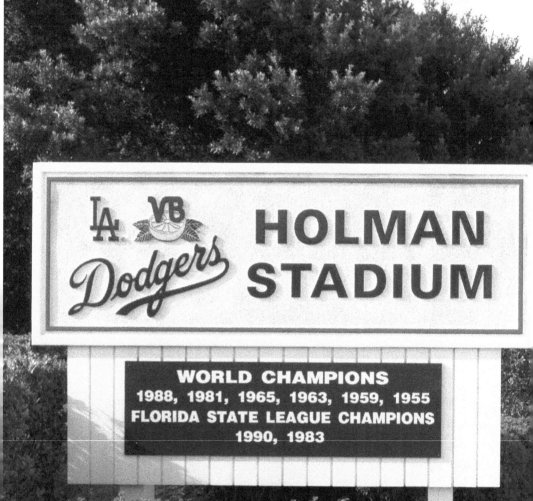

Holman Stadium/Dodgertown, spring training site for the Los Angeles Dodgers in Vero Beach, Florida, until 2008

THE ROAD TO DODGERTOWN

"You! Come with me!" Tommy Lasorda shouted. The legendary manager of the Los Angeles Dodgers led the six-foot-four rookie away from his minor league drills to the main stadium at Dodgertown, in Vero Beach, Florida, where spring training was underway for the major league team.

Batting practice was in full swing, and as a nineteen-year-old pitcher, David felt a brief stab of shock and self-doubt when he realized the batters he would be facing were perennial all-stars, already borderline Hall of Famers at the top of the Dodger lineup. For a moment he could barely breathe. He short-armed his first pitch and threw it at Ron Cey's head, and Cey had to hit the ground for safety. As Cey glared, David reminded himself that he was the Dodgers' number one draft pick that year. He remembered the extraordinary efforts the scout had made to recruit him, the unusual contract he and his father had negotiated with the Dodgers. Most importantly, the confidence he had harnessed since childhood came rushing back. His brown eyes focused on home plate, and as he recognized the next four players, he knew which pitch to try on each one. On that first sunny day of spring training in Florida, he erased the memory of Cey's glare and pitched well to baseball greats Steve Garvey,

Reggie Smith, Davey Lopes, and Bill Russell. It was a good day in Dodgertown.

Dreams of a place like Dodgertown began before David knew what the road to major league baseball would mean. Waking up at 4 a.m., spending ten hours a day, seven days a week, at the field, and earning a small salary weren't part of his boyhood visions of the sport he loved. He was a natural athlete, the star of his Little League team in Bel Air, Maryland, about thirty miles northeast of Baltimore. The local paper, *The Aegis*, featured him at age eleven on the cover, touting the pitcher as the best in the league. Baseball looked like a fun and easy path to success.

David's brother, Bob, was four years older, and sports created a strong bond between the siblings. It was part of the family DNA. Their father, Warren Lesch, was an avid follower of baseball and football and an excellent tennis player, and he believed in the importance of playing a sport. Many neighbors in the Howard Park development in Bel Air had manicured lawns and carefully maintained gardens, but the Lesch family turned their backyard into a sports field. Margaret Lesch loved her role as homemaker and mother and also played an important part in the sports world that dominated the modest home on Brooks Road. Depending on whether it was baseball or football season, she carefully measured out distances in the yard, creating accurate lines for the makeshift fields with white flour from bags she kept in the kitchen for baking.

There were only four streets in the housing development, around eighty homes in all, with lots of neighborhood children ready to kick footballs or pitch baseballs in the Lesch family's yard. Bob and David could ride their bikes or walk to St. Margaret School, and there were nearby woods and a lake to explore. In the 1960s, the darker sides of the bigger world had not penetrated this small Maryland town.

Television was a new luxury in those days, and David and Bob especially liked *The American Sportsman*, a popular family show starring Curt Gowdy as host and hero. He took the boys—along with the show's celebrity guests like Bing Crosby—on flyfishing trips in the Andes, hunting adventures in Africa, and exotic journeys across the globe, thanks to a small black and white console that sat on a modest credenza in the living room. The show's theme song, opening with "Follow me, and find contentment," was an anthem in the Lesch household. Sometimes when fried chicken appeared on the table for dinner, everyone pretended they were American sportsmen and the meal was the result of a successful hunt in some faraway place.

Warren Lesch—tall and athletic, with prematurely gray hair worn in a flattop—had always wanted to be a doctor. His father worked in the New Jersey plant of General Motors, and Warren was the first in his family to attend college, graduating with a degree in chemistry from Monmouth College. He was quick to realize that the cost of medical schools on the East Coast was beyond his family's means, but a fortuitous transfer for his father to Dallas brought Warren an unexpected opportunity. He discovered that the University of Texas Southwestern Medical School offered free tuition to state residents. As soon as he could officially claim residency, he enrolled, graduated with honors, completed his internship, and began his residency at St. Rita's Hospital in the small town of Lima, Ohio.

While Warren was attending Monmouth, he met Margaret Marie Corres, a petite brunette who worked as an operator at New Jersey Bell Telephone Company (later acquired by AT&T), on a blind date. Her father's family had emigrated from Spain, and her mother was Irish. Marge was born and raised in Newark, New Jersey, where her father worked as an electrician. The family was poor, and ethnic tensions in the 1940s made her childhood

An abandoned 1950s lab at the US Army's Aberdeen Proving Ground

difficult. At a young age, she found solace in religion and was a devout Roman Catholic her entire life. She also was a music prodigy and was invited to play the piano at Carnegie Hall when she was in her teens. Her personality reflected a special harmony that her family and friends cherished. Marge and Warren married in 1955, and Robert was born on September 30, 1956, in Lima. After completing his residency, Warren joined the Army as a medical doctor and completed his basic training at Fort Sam Houston in San Antonio, a city that would ironically become home base for David many decades later. After basic training Warren was stationed at the Edgewood Arsenal, part of the Aberdeen Proving Ground in Maryland.

Established in 1917, Aberdeen conducted research, manufactured chemical agents, and tested, stored, and disposed of toxic materials. Between 1955 and 1975 the US Army Chemical Corps carried out classified medical studies at the Edgewood Arsenal with the purpose of evaluating the impact of low-dose chemical warfare agents on military personnel and testing protective clothing and pharmaceuticals.

The Department of Defense reports that seven thousand soldiers took part in experiments that involved exposures to more than 250 different chemicals. In 1990 the Edgewood area of Aberdeen was added to the EPA's National Priorities List of the country's most serious uncontrolled or abandoned hazardous waste sites requiring longtime remediation. After the terrorist attacks of September 11, 2001, the chemical weapons stored in the Edgewood chemical activity depot were put on an elimination schedule, and all were destroyed by 2006.

In the late 1950s Warren worked on some of the top-secret chemical warfare projects underway there, but he never brought stories about the dangers home. Many years later he confided to his family that he felt guilty about that work. He was acutely aware of both the Hippocratic oath to heal, which he had taken as a physician, and of the horrible effects of the nerve gases, sarin, mustard agent, and psychoactive agents like LSD he had studied in the Edgewood Arsenal.

He was relieved when his stint in the Army ended and was excited to start his practice as a family physician in Bel Air. His took a deep personal interest in his patients, enjoyed making house calls, and never charged patients who were experiencing difficult financial circumstances. He and Margaret welcomed their second son, David, on September 14, 1960, and their family life pretty much resembled *The Adventures of Ozzie and Harriet* television show that was so popular in the 1950s and 1960s. Family dinner every night at six o'clock, regular attendance at the neighborhood Catholic church, vacations at the New Jersey shore, Little League games, and visits to grandparents in Texas created a stability that provided David with the moral compass he would need in his adult life. Warren never dreamed that decades later his son would face challenges where that compass would be crucial to his survival or that someday he would experience firsthand the effects of some of those dangerous chemicals his father had studied at the Aberdeen Proving Ground.

But in the mid-1960s David's adventures focused on sledding down the nearby hills in the winter with his childhood friend and neighbor, Doug Reitz, and baseball once the snow melted. Doug remembers that David was "the most feared pitcher in Little League baseball. He could throw the ball so hard. Getting even a base hit off him was a miracle. He was the go-to person when the game was on the line; he was as graceful as a gazelle and totally unaware of how talented he was."

In high school David added basketball to his sports career. He was voted Most Valuable Player his sophomore, junior, and senior years at the John Carroll School, the first student at the private Catholic school to achieve that accolade three years in a row, but it came at a cost. Dedication to basketball and baseball extracted emotional energy, and there was little time to make the social connections that usually occur in high school. David was shy and also self-conscious about the big-rimmed glasses he had worn since second grade. His closest friends were other boys on the teams, mostly older, who graduated before he did. He played sandlot sports with his brother Bob and friends when he wasn't at school, but he was always the youngest player, yet one of the best.

Kevin Birchen, now an account manager at BeiGene, an

international cancer research company, met David at high school basketball practice. "I recognized David's skill level immediately," he says, "and his kindness. I lived in Jarrettsville, a small farming community about forty-five minutes away, and all my friends attended the local public school. I felt a little bit like an outsider at John Carroll and was one of just three African American students there. But David and I immediately found common ground through sports. We both saw value in competition and the resilience it generates." The boys went in different directions after high school but reconnected at a chance meeting in Boston decades later. "We had lunch together, and it was as if no years had passed. Our conversation picked up as if we had spoken the day before. He asked how I was doing in terms of the racial issues that were prevalent in Boston at the time and wanted to hear my experiences and hopes for the future, listening with care to everything I said. His ability to truly listen is, and always has been, unique."

During his high school years, David may not have always listened carefully in class. Academics were not his top priority. He did well in classes he liked—history, social studies, and English—and made average grades in classes that did not interest him. The pocket calculator had just been invented, but of course that new device was not allowed in math class, so David barely passed geometry and calculus. It was the 1970s: the era of disco music, bell-bottoms, and recreational drugs that popular bands like Earth, Wind & Fire touted in their songs. David experimented with it all, and at fifteen he and a good friend began to frequent a local nightclub, proud of their cleverness and enjoying the illicit fun. Since Maryland driver's licenses did not have photographs in the 1970s, it was easy to borrow an older classmate's current or expired license.

The dimly lit lounge and scantily clad young women with big breasts and long bare legs offered the thrill of forbidden adventure. The boys worked on their adult impersonations, trying to emulate the middle-aged men sipping drinks at small cocktail tables in the early evening, sometimes giving way to giggles of nervous astonishment at what they saw.

One morning David and his nightclub partner in crime decided to drink Jack Daniels before school. They stumbled into their physics class, turned around, and raced to the school bathroom to throw up. The nurse took pity on them, sending them home and pretending to believe they both had food poisoning. Many years later David would experience a real poisoning, but in 1975 Jack Daniels was the dangerous drink that made him sick, and he never tried the Tennessee whiskey again.

The school's AP English teacher had been a student of Albert Einstein at Princeton University. David and his classmates considered the fifty-year-old an ancient relic. Mr. Canoun's science-fiction class was considered one of the most difficult at The John Carroll School, but it changed David's scholastic trajectory. He loved the course and chose Arthur C. Clarke's iconic 1968 novelization of *2001: A Space Odyssey* for his essay and oral presentation. Canoun was impressed, awarding him an A-plus and comparing his work to a doctoral dissertation from Johns Hopkins University that he had read. The praise was a catalyst, and David found a new confidence in academics, matching the confidence he had always experienced in sports. But that did not halt the fun he created with misbehavior that lasted through some of his college years.

David watched the television series *Star Trek* as a teenager. His wild days in high school and beyond would later remind him of a favorite episode, "Tapestry," in *Star Trek: The Next*

Generation, the sequel to the original series. Jean-Luc Picard, the captain of the Starship *Enterprise*, is shot by something that hits his heart. His recovery is complicated by the fact that he has an artificial heart, implanted during his rebellious youth. The omnipotent recurring character Q appears in Picard's subconscious, and he thinks he has entered the afterlife. He confesses that a fight he instigated as a young Star Fleet cadet necessitated his artificial heart, telling Q he wishes he could take back the whole experience and use diplomacy to solve the problem. Q snaps his fingers and sends Picard back in time, where he uses diplomacy to prevent a battle. When Q snaps his fingers again to transport Picard to the present, the hero is only an ensign, not the captain of the starship. Q explains that indiscretions and dubious behavior are essential parts of growth and encourages Picard to take chances in life in order to advance beyond the status quo. With the lesson learned, Picard is restored as captain of the *Enterprise*.

David would incorporate both scenarios from the episode into his life, daring to take risks but also harnessing the art of diplomacy to tackle some of the world's most challenging conflicts. But in 1978, as a high school senior, his biggest challenge was the decision about his immediate future. There was a flurry of recruitment by colleges offering basketball scholarships. The US Naval Academy pursued him aggressively, recognizing his athleticism as a sharp-shooting wing and forward. But at only six feet and three inches, he realized he was short for those basketball positions—though he would grow another inch in college—and he knew he didn't have the expert dribbling skills to be a guard. More importantly, he really wanted to play baseball. He recognized his growing talent as a pitcher, and he knew he had the arm.

First love also came calling. Lisa Schaefert was both the head cheerleader at The John Carroll School and David's lab partner in physics class. Her beauty and brains intimidated him, but they were friends, and Lisa helped him get through the final semester of a course made even more difficult by misadventures like the Jack Daniels embarrassment. After graduation David learned that Lisa was interested in being more than friends. She told him he was handsome, which is always a great start toward romance. He wondered if it had to do with his new contact lenses.

While experiencing all the exciting demands of a tempestuous new relationship, David felt the powerful pull of baseball. During the summer he joined the league of sixteen- to nineteen-year-olds and played for Mike's Auto Mart team in Baltimore. Part of the All-American Amateur Baseball Association, the respected team produced quite a few players who were drafted by major league baseball teams. The assistant coach, Jim Gilbert, was also a scout for the Baltimore Orioles, and as early as 1978 eyes were on David as a potential candidate for professional ball. Mike's Auto Mart team did well that summer, finishing just behind another Baltimore team called Johnny's, the perennial national champion that would recruit David the following summer.

Balancing the demands of baseball practice and games with the emotional rollercoaster of dating was a challenge that David met with the courage of youth, mixed with some angst. Lisa was blonde, blue-eyed, beautiful, and athletic, and as the head cheerleader she was one of the most sought-after girls at school. David was surprised when she was attracted to him and became his girlfriend. That summer, like most college-bound teenagers, the couple wondered how their lives would change. They went to movies and drank whiskey at the Draft Board, a local watering hole established during the Vietnam War, when being drafted was a strong possibility for the country's young men. Lisa already had turned eighteen—the legal drinking age in Maryland at the time—and David continued to use the same altered license that had given him access to other forbidden places.

In fall 1978 Lisa went to Georgetown University in Washington, DC, and David enrolled at Western Maryland College (now McDaniel College), a short drive away. The movie *National Lampoon's Animal House* had been the hit of the summer, a comedy starring John Belushi as a college student determined to take fraternity life to new heights of trouble and hilarity. David, his roommate and high school friend Dave Sutor, and the rest of the students in the freshman dormitory had a blueprint for misadventure. The first night on campus, a group lit a bonfire in the middle of the quad of the main dorm. They threw dorm furniture into the fire along with trash cans filled with grain alcohol. The fire department was called, and David's college life began in a blaze of glory.

Both David and Dave made the varsity baseball team as freshmen. Most of the other players were upperclassmen who became mentors and lifelong friends. The last game of the season was against Johns Hopkins University. Goose Gosselin was scheduled to pitch, but he developed arm soreness, and the coach asked David if he could pitch. He jumped at the chance, although he had started a game only four days earlier, which is considered a short time to rest before playing again. It was a lucky day for David. Walter Youse, the general manager from Johnny's, was there to scout other players. When he saw the freshman pitch a complete game three-hit shutout, he asked if he would play for Johnny's in the upcoming summer season.

For more than two decades Johnny's had won almost every

David Lesch pitching for Johnny's, 1979

national championship. Some great players had been part of the legendary team, including Hall of Famers Reggie Jackson and Al Kaline. And Youse was not only the team's general manager but he was also a scout for the Milwaukee Brewers. Of course David accepted the offer, and in summer 1979 he became the team's top pitcher, helping Johnny's earn its way to another national championship.

The final game was against a New Orleans team, and David pitched the last five innings, including the final out, a fly ball to center field, to win the championship. Before that triumph, a different batter hit a ground ball to the second baseman, who threw to first for what seemed like the final out. Everyone piled on David at the pitcher's mound, thinking the game was won. But the first-base umpire ruled the batter safe, saying the first baseman had taken his foot off the bag too soon. The players had to brush themselves off, compose themselves, and face the next batter, who hit the final fly ball out. Life lessons like these, honed on the baseball diamond, would later be useful in ways David could never have imagined in 1979.

He was approached by scouts from a variety of colleges, including the University of Texas, Stanford University, and the University of Florida, encouraging him to transfer from Western Maryland College. But Walter Youse urged him to attend Central Arizona College in the fall, a junior college that would allow him to be drafted much sooner than if he attended a four-year college. He mentioned that the Brewers already were interested in recruiting David and that they often stashed potential draft picks at Central Arizona. David recognized the proverbial fork in the road. He would be more than two thousand miles away from his family and Lisa, and the school did not have the prominent reputation of other universities that were pursuing him. But he trusted Youse.

In fall 1979 he traveled from Baltimore to Coolidge, Arizona. The flight to Phoenix was the longest airplane trip he had ever taken. Family, friends, and Lisa watched him depart. There were tears at the airport as David answered the irresistible siren call of baseball.

Sonoran Desert, Arizona

WELCOME TO MARS

As the DC-10 flew toward Sky Harbor Airport, passengers saw a dust devil whirl across a desert of blowing sand and swoop into the narrow canyons below. Granite mountains loomed blood red in the setting sun. The pilot announced that the temperature in Phoenix was 118 degrees and advised passengers to expect some turbulence during the flight's last twenty minutes because of the extreme heat. David was glad that his brother Bob had accompanied him on this two-thousand-mile journey, the farthest he had ever traveled from home. Looking out the window at the landscape below, he imagined he was aboard Starship *Enterprise*, landing on another planet with his sibling by his side. Perhaps they had discovered Mars. Sky Harbor was a perfect name for its airport.

That first impression would intensify as they drove south toward Central Arizona College, through the Gila River Indian Community, where sunbaked brown fields and adobe huts hinted at a tribal history that once included master craftsmen and farmers. It would be several decades before a heritage center showcasing ancestral treasures and lavish hotel-casinos were built, changing the Mars-like desert into something still more otherworldly.

In 1979 the hour-long drive to Coolidge took the brothers

through the Sacaton Mountains, where Ira Hayes, the Pima Native American Marine who assisted in raising the US flag on Iwo Jima, had grown up. The rocky hills of granite, desert saguaro and cholla, and relentless heat certainly toughened Hayes for battles he faced in World War II, and the baseball "boot camp" in Coolidge would do the same for David. National news stations declared Coolidge the hottest place in the country in 1979 and Bob was delighted to return to Maryland the next day.

That same year national news covered three extraordinary international developments unfolding on the other side of the globe, events that would change the Middle East and the world. Most American teenagers like David, and many adults, were only vaguely aware of them. But they were familiar with the long lines at gas stations, an inconvenience to drivers of all ages. They stretched for blocks, and occasional fights broke out when people tried to cut in line. There was a shortage of plastic gas containers as hoarders recognized that fuel had become a precious commodity.

The important backstory linked to US fuel shortages was the Iranian Revolution, which was taking place in a country that produced a large quantity of the world's oil and impacted markets just as the Arab-Israeli War had done in 1973. In February 1979 the Ayatollah Ruhollah Khomeini, an Islamic revolutionary and religious leader, left his exile in Paris and returned to Tehran, effectively ending the rule of Mohammad Reza Pahlavi, known by most Westerners as the Shah of Iran. With the pro-West Shah's departure, Iranian oil production dipped, and the Organization of the Petroleum Exporting Countries (OPEC) raised it prices. American drivers felt the sting personally, described well by the title of Princeton University historian Meg Jacobs's book *Panic at the Pump*. Later that year Iranian militants seized the US embassy in Tehran and took fifty-two Americans hostage. These events spurred public interest in the Persian Gulf nation, which most Americans, until then, could not locate on a map of the Middle East.

The region also attracted worldwide attention when the Egypt-Israel peace treaty was signed by Israeli prime minister Menachem Begin and Egyptian president Anwar Sadat. In March 1979, with US president Jimmy Carter looking on, the two avowed enemies met at Camp David in Maryland to complete what appeared to be a huge step toward peace in the Middle East. While an achievement in and of itself, as the first peace agreement between Israel and an Arab state, it was an imperfect one. It outlined two frameworks for peace—one dealing with Egyptian-Israeli relations and the other with the issue of Palestine—but they were not organically linked. And there was little, if any, progress on the Palestinian front—a failure that has repeatedly caused terrible tragedies over the decades, including the horrific invasion of Israel by Hamas on October 7, 2023, the subsequent Israeli military retribution in the Gaza Strip, and ongoing turmoil in surrounding regions.

William Quandt, a member of the National Security Council in the Carter administration, was directly involved in the 1979 negotiations at Camp David. Years later he and David became colleagues and friends. Looking back at the agreement, Quandt recalled that the leaders involved felt such animosity toward each other that they sent messages from separate rooms via emissaries, explaining that "it was the best deal we could get at the time."

That winter the Soviet invasion of Afghanistan added more drama and political complexity to a tumultuous year. In his State of the Union address in January 1980, Carter urged Americans to pay attention to these events, to look beyond US borders, and to recognize that "it has never been more clear that the state of our union depends on the state of the world."

Two decades later David worked closely with the Carter Center, a nonprofit organization founded in 1982 to advance human rights worldwide. His interactions with the former president were substantial and personally meaningful, and their shared goals for peace are reflected in the photos and personal notes that line David's office wall today. His 2001 book, *1979: The Year That Shaped the Modern Middle East*, probes the ramifications of the Iranian Revolution, the Egypt-Israel peace treaty, and the Soviet invasion of Afghanistan—major events that were occurring when David was a young athlete focusing on baseball. It concludes with a warning of sorts: "Gazing down from the mountain peaks of history, one might perceive the world as either better or worse after the tumult of 1979, but one could not deny that it was different. The Middle East, indeed the world, had changed—we just didn't know it yet."

In 1979 David was part of that majority of Americans still unaware of the big changes on the world stage. But he clearly realized that his own world would never be the same when he arrived at Central Arizona College. During orientation students were advised to avoid visits to the laundry room or vending machines at night because rattlesnakes liked to warm their bodies on the asphalt walking paths. Coyotes and mountain lions were also frequent nocturnal visitors. Five days a week the college's baseball team began the day with a run up the small mountain adjacent to campus. Practice took place in the scorching heat, and pitchers ran an additional five to ten miles when practice concluded, trotting along a desert path that looked like a Martian landscape. During afternoon runs the small group of pitchers often saw the bones of some dead animal. Their standing joke was that someday they would discover the bones of a former team pitcher.

The head coach was Kenny Richardson, an ex-Marine who was respected for his toughness. Known as KR, he used several special training methods that seemed torturous to his players. He would bellow "Dive!" after hitting ground balls to infielders to teach them not to be afraid of the dirt. He liked to set up the pitching machine on the mound, calibrating it at eighty-five miles an hour and directing hitters to stand on home plate and absorb the pitches on their chests while yelling a primal scream. His plan was to banish all fear of fastballs, but the exercise sometimes produced the opposite effect, eliciting a stream of curses from KR.

Recreation in the middle of the desert was limited. David and his best friend at school, Scott Orlich from Butte, Montana, sometimes went into Phoenix on the weekends. They cruised East Camelback Road sometimes stopping at a restaurant or dive bar or crashing college parties at Arizona State University in Scottsdale. A bunch of eighteen- and nineteen-year-old males full of testosterone were destined for trouble when drinking, sometimes experimenting with peyote, and inventing their own diversions. One night a group of players decided to hunt for jackrabbits with shotguns. They drove into the desert in pickup trucks, illuminating their prey with headlights. They sat in the truck beds and took turns shooting while the others rode in the truck cabs.

David was riding in the passenger seat when the driver took a sharp turn and a shooter in the back fell off the tailgate. The fall caused him to accidentally shoot his gun, and the pellets whizzed by the truck's cab, taking off the side mirror right next to David's "golden arm." After gasping at the close call and realizing that David's baseball career could have ended if his arm were a few inches outside the window, the group continued its adventure. They cut the heads off the rabbits they killed and hung them from the doors of rooms of teammates who had remained behind. They devised an even more diabolical plan with a few remaining heads, placing them inside the receptacle area of a candy vending machine, just out of sight. The next morning a female student reached in for her candy and pulled out a bloody head. Her scream echoed through the halls and still lingers in David's memory, along with regret.

As the season progressed, scouts for major league baseball teams began to attend practices. KR would frequently direct David to run in the desert or work out in the weight room while the scouts were there. It dawned on him that the coach was hiding him, but KR eventually came to David's room and explained. The Milwaukee Brewers, the team that KR favored and not so secretly worked for, hoped to acquire David in the January or June 1980 drafts, and KR did not want the other teams' scouts to see him pitch. He told David he had already caught the eye of Brewers manager George Bamberger. While it was gratifying to know that his coach thought highly of him and the Brewers wanted him, it was also frustrating to be kept out of the bigger recruiting game. David needn't have worried. The seasoned recruiters had their own creative ways around KR's guard over him.

A West Coast scout from the Baltimore Orioles found someone at the college who knew David and devised a way to talk to him. The mutual friend told him an MLB scout wanted to contact him but could not call on his dorm telephone because the lines, as the Orioles scout surmised, were probably bugged by KR. He asked David what his uncle's name was, explaining that the scout would call the dorm telephone using that name, a signal for David to hurry to a nearby pay phone where the scout would call him.

The plan worked. "Uncle Tom" called the dorm and David went to a pay phone to speak with the scout, who wanted to see him pitch before recommending him to the Orioles. He suggested an unusual way to make this happen without KR's knowledge. David would go on his usual ten-mile run in the desert, where a helicopter would pick him up and fly him to nearby Casa Grande, a town with an MLB training facility where the scout could watch him pitch.

The pursuit of David Lesch had begun. One MLB team offered to send women to his dorm room. He declined but was impressed by the diversity of recruitment techniques. The scouts got wind of what was going on soon enough. One day as David and Scott were walking back to the clubhouse after training, they heard a loud whistle. It was an older man who waved to the boys, pointed to a pile of pebbles, and left. Under the pebbles David found a note addressed to him, asking him to go to the bullpen area the next day at 4 p.m. sharp and start pitching. The note explained that the man was the West Coast scout for the Los Angeles Dodgers.

The next day David took a catcher to the bullpen and positioned himself near the left field fence. He began throwing the ball and heard a whisper from the bushes bordering the fence. The scout was hiding there. He instructed David to pitch some fastballs, curves, and changeups and asked him to demonstrate what he would throw in specific situations. "It's 0–2 on Rod Carew, what are you going to throw?" the scout whispered. David knew Carew was a perennial all-star and one of the best hitters in MLB history. He threw a fastball up and in to the catcher, who was chuckling with delight at this strange clandestine test. David aced it, and the Los Angeles Dodgers chose him as their number one pick in their January 1980 winter baseball draft.

After receiving one of the most exciting telephone calls of his life from the Dodgers, David discussed the offer with his father, slightly torn between finishing college and hoping for an offer the following year or playing professional baseball immediately. Warren Lesch called Cal Ripken Sr., a top coach with the Orioles, father of Hall of Famer Cal Ripken Jr., and an acquaintance,

Pro Baseball

Lesch First Round Pick Of Dodgers

Pitched For John Carroll, Johnny's

The Los Angeles Dodgers made former John Carroll two-sport star Dave Lesch their Number 1 pick in baseball's Winter Free Agent Draft Tuesday.

Lesch, who last Summer pitched Johnny's to the 16-19 AAABA national championship, was the tenth player chosen in the draft and now has six months to decide whether he wants to sign with the Dodgers.

The 19-year old flamethrower was reportedly high on the shopping list of at least two other major league teams—Milwaukee and Baltimore—but was scarfed up by the Dodgers, who are seeking to rebound from their worst finish in over a decade.

Lesch blossomed as a major league prospect two Summers ago when he played for Mike's Auto Mart, the second best amateur team in the Baltimore area. Then, after a year at Western Maryland College, the lanky righthander put together some impressive statistics with Johnny's last Summer. The Baltimore-based amateur team is annually one of the best clubs in the nation, having copped the AAABA title nine times in the 35-years of the Johnstown (Pa.) tournament's existence.

Also, Johnny's has sent a total of 24 players to the big leagues including Al Kaline, Reggie Jackson, Butch Wynegar, Moose Haas and Willie Mays Aikens.

Lesch, who spent this past Fall at Central Arizona Junior College, has said he will sign with the Dodgers "if the offer is a reasonable one."

If the Dodgers do not sign the Bel Air teenager by June, his name will go back into the free agent list and he will be eligible to be drafted again by any of the major league clubs.

DAVE LESCH

since their sons had competed against each other in high school. He asked if David, who was in Bel Air for the Christmas break, should sign with the Dodgers or go back to school for another year. Ripkin told him the Dodgers were a top-notch organization and reminded him that being drafted number one should not be taken lightly. There was a chance that if David stayed at school it might not happen again.

KR was furious about it all, and a profanity-laced telephone call with David followed. The unpleasantness made the decision easy. David signed with the Dodgers, and his father negotiated the deal. The days of big signing bonuses had not yet arrived, and Warren proposed that instead of negotiating for a large signing bonus the Dodgers would pay the tuition for any college David might attend post-baseball. The Dodgers liked the idea, knowing full well that most of those drafted never went back to college. They never imagined that their star pitcher would go on to earn bachelor's, master's, and doctoral degrees in the years ahead.

For now, Dodgertown was David's future, and he greeted it with gusto, delighted to leave the harsh desert behind for a lush and balmy Vero Beach, Florida. It was there that Tommy Lasorda put him through the pitching test against baseball greats Ron Cey, Steve Garvey, Reggie Smith, Davey Lopes, and Bill Russell. The successful outcome on that nerve-wracking first day of training in January 1980 triggered a self-confidence and courage that have prevailed through disappointments and grand achievements on the baseball diamond, in war zones, and in the shifting landscapes of political diplomacy and personal relationships. An early disappointment came at the end of spring training, when David stepped into a hole while he was running sprints and wrenched his lower back. Immobile for five days, he saw his chance of breaking camp with the High-A club in Vero Beach slip away and realized he was destined to join a Low-A club in Canada.

Before he headed to Alberta, he faced more than a month of rehab in Vero Beach, where he rented a house with two other players. One grew marijuana in the house as a side business. The other dated a private detective who was an alligator hunter and drug user. She was a tall buxom blonde, hard looking, with a face that reflected the tough life she lived. She was also a thief, and when she stole some money from her boyfriend, he called the police. The officers arrived at the house to investigate, walking past the other roommate's marijuana crop. Everyone held their breath, aware of the dire consequences the discovery would create. David found the entire situation disturbing and couldn't wait to get down to the business of baseball.

When he finished rehab in May he was assigned to the Dodgers' minor league team based in Lethbridge, located in southern Alberta. Part of the Pioneer Baseball League, it was comprised of teams in Canada, Montana, and Idaho. He rented a basement apartment with a teammate and plunged into rigorous training. Just before the season began, he developed ulnar nerve palsy in his pitching arm, a result of the added pressure he put on his arm to compensate for his still-painful lower back. Weakness in the arm and tenderness in the elbow joint are the last thing a pitcher wants. The diagnosis put him on the injured list for the second time in less than a year. He was out for more than half the summer but traveled with the team on long bus rides, ranging from Calgary to Helena to Idaho Falls for games.

During games he sat in the bullpen with the other pitchers, and to kill time the young men devised a game of sorts. They would look for a good-looking woman in the stands and enlist the help of a young fan by giving him a baseball along with a note to be delivered to her, asking if she wanted to meet after the game. David never participated, and the ploy usually did not meet with success. One night during a game in Helena a particularly gorgeous young woman was in the crowd. She was blonde, had a perfect build, and was obviously used to attention. Almost everyone in the bullpen sent notes to her, but she did not respond to any of them. She came over to the bullpen during the latter part of the game and pointed at David, announcing she was only interested in him because he was the only player who did not send her a note. Her name was Cara. Recognizing that a long-term relationship was not possible, since they lived in different cities and David was headed home at the end of the season, they became good friends. Whenever a game was scheduled in Helena or a nearby town in Montana, they dated, and while he had temporarily lost access to the pitcher's mound, he had won a girlfriend who appreciated the fact that he had not pursued her with a note.

Midway through the season he got to play against the Butte Copper Kings in Lethbridge. They were the league's Brewer franchise, coached by none other than KR, David's former coach. Several old friends, including Scott Orlich, were on the team. David was put in late in the game with his team trailing 13–1. When he went to the mound to pitch, KR put himself in the game as his team's third-base coach and began to yell and curse at the pitcher he had once coached.

David's teammates were astonished. The third baseman and the catcher came out to the pitching mound and hatched a plan. There was a runner on third base, and David pretended he was going to pick him off. Instead of throwing the ball to his third baseman, he threw it directly at KR in the coach's box. It went off perfectly, hitting KR in the legs. When KR sprinted angrily toward David, he was tackled by the third baseman. Both teams' benches emptied, followed by pushing and shoving, in a spirit of fun. Most of the players on the Copper Kings team loved it, and everyone met for beers and laughs when the game was over.

David's Lethbridge Dodgers were the best in the league, and when they won the 1980 championship several players made it to the majors. Although he received a championship ring, David realized he had virtually nothing to do with the big win. It was the first time in his life that he had not been the star of the team, and it was a strange feeling.

Early the next year David returned to Dodgertown for his second spring-training season. He had worked out consistently in the off-season and reported to practice in excellent shape. During batting practice, as he was picking up some balls in the outfield as pitchers usually do, baseball great Sandy Koufax spotted him and shouted, "David, don't pick up another ball until you say hi to me!" Koufax had been a roving pitching instructor during David's first spring training and was one of David's heroes. Being greeted by name by the "Left Arm of God" was an extraordinary start to the season.

David's first appearance on the pitcher's mound at the main stadium was stellar. His fastball registered ninety-five miles per hour on the JUGS radar gun, and he pitched three innings of no-hit ball with several strikeouts of top-level players. He was ecstatic, finally pitching the way he wanted, injury free, and enjoying the compliments from Dodgers head pitching coach Ron Perranoski. His next start was against the Minnesota Twins at their spring-training complex. In warm-ups he had trouble getting his shoulder loose, and there was some pain. His fastball was five or ten miles slower than usual, but he was determined to overcome the problem.

During the rest of spring training and extended spring training in St. Petersburg on Florida's Gulf Coast, David's pitching was inconsistent, depending on how his shoulder felt. Eventually diagnosed as a rotator cuff problem, the injury was a rollercoaster ride performance-wise. Unfortunately surgery was not then advanced enough to repair rotator cuff problems. Ironically it would be the team physician for the Dodgers, orthopedic surgeon Frank Jobe, who would introduce new shoulder surgery techniques in 1990, a decade too late for David.

That spring he lived with two other injured Dodger teammates on Treasure Island, known for its miles of white sand beaches and glistening turquoise water. But as beautiful as the setting was, it felt like purgatory to David. He feared that he was earmarked for a return to Lethbridge, which was a very disappointing prospect to a young man whose dream was to be a major league baseball pitcher. Toward the end of the season the manager, Gary LaRocque, called David into his office and asked him to assess his recent pitching performance. With customary honesty he told LaRocque that it had been below his expectations. What followed were some of the hardest words to hear in baseball. David's manager told him that he was being released from his contract. He took the news bravely, thanked LaRocque, and walked out into the Florida sunshine.

David had no doubt that he would complete his college degree and at no cost thanks to the contract his father had negotiated with the Dodgers. Ideas for areas of study began to percolate in David's mind. History and the art of negotiation fascinated him, and the confidence he had developed on the baseball diamond fueled his optimism.

Recently reunited with his girlfriend Lisa, David invited her to join him in Orlando to close this big chapter in his life. Before he headed back to Bel Air and a new start, he took her to Walt Disney World, which was celebrating its tenth anniversary. With abandon that's only possible in the Magic Kingdom, they explored Adventureland and Tomorrowland, where they rode the famous rocket to Mars. EPCOT Center was under construction, and the Spaceship Earth pavilion was nearly complete. Future World was in the early stages of development, but it was full of exciting promise, and David Lesch felt similar optimism about his path ahead.

Lesch family home in Bel Air, Maryland, and family portrait (from left): Bob, Margaret, Warren, and David

CURVEBALLS

Over the next five years life took some unexpected twists and turns. Leaving Dodgertown for academia, David began a measured march toward a new and larger playing field. Brilliant mentors, a tumultuous marriage, a first-time visit to the Arab world, and a tragic fiery blaze were the catalysts for a journey that would transport him to presidential palaces and the war zones of the Middle East.

But during summer 1981 that journey had just begun. He was comfortably ensconced in his childhood home in Bel Air. His mother's prayers were answered: her twenty-year-old son was under her roof again. He couldn't wait for her to cook his favorite foods and take care of his laundry, two perks he had not enjoyed for nearly two years. His old bedroom was the same as the day he left. Baseball, basketball, football, and tennis trophies still lined the wood-paneled walls, and his mahogany desk was ready for the college assignments ahead. In September he enrolled at University of Maryland, Baltimore County (UMBC), a satellite campus of the University of Maryland at College Park. He chose it partly because his brother Bob was the sports information director for the athletics program and partly because it was an easy drive from home.

A college tour through the state of Maryland would reveal several dozen centuries-old colleges and universities with breathtaking colonial architecture and a plethora of red brick. Washington College, St. John's College, the US Naval Academy, Johns Hopkins University, and others exude prestige and power. Four of the founders of St. John's College signed the Declaration of Independence. A later graduate named Francis Scott Key wrote "The Star-Spangled Banner" in 1814. UMBC was a latecomer and lacked the famous alumni—other than the actress Kathleen Turner—and Palladian grandeur of those much older schools, but it was the first public college or university in Maryland to be inclusive of all races. Its student enrollment was just 750, and there were only 45 faculty members when it opened its doors in 1966. The campus consisted of three buildings, and one had a rather chilling history that fascinated its students, including David when he arrived in 1981.

To create the UMBC campus, the University of Maryland's Board of Regents approved the acquisition of 435 acres through a donation from Spring Grove State Hospital. Founded in 1797, Spring Grove is the second-oldest psychiatric hospital in the United States. In 1921 its leadership constructed an impressive three-story, red-brick building, dominating the still-rural landscape. It was the country's first facility designed specifically for the care and treatment of mentally ill prisoners. Nicknamed the "Criminal Building," the Hillcrest Building would inspire ghoulish legends as the years passed, and students at UMBC added their own macabre stories of deranged murderers whose ghosts wandered around the campus. Late-night parties at UMBC usually concluded with dramatic warnings to be alert, predicting dire sequels to the ghost stories children hear at summer camp. Thankfully there was a reassuring hero on campus. A marble statue of a Chesapeake retriever—Maryland's state dog—stood guard in the quad. The first class at the new college chose "True Grit" as their mascot. Students who worried about the horrors of the Hillcrest Building or their grades or anything else had only to rub his marble nose to ensure safety and good luck.

When David arrived at the school in 1981, enrollment had climbed to 5,800 students, and the infamous Hillcrest Building was serving as the student union. He rubbed the nose of True Grit and dabbled briefly with the idea of pursuing sports medicine until two remarkable professors introduced him to a path as compelling as baseball had once been.

Louis Cantori was a highly respected Middle East scholar who also loved sports, especially the Orioles. According to David, he did not look like a professor or act like one. He was a former Marine, gruff looking with a garrulous voice. He dressed in jeans and a white button-down shirt rolled up at the sleeves. But he was very much the intellectual who could quote the famous philosophers and the current batting averages of Orioles players.

Cantori's class, electrifying in its intensity, examined dramatic current events and evolving international relations theories. Just as it is now, the Middle East was a hot spot in the early 1980s. The Iran-Iraq War, the Israeli invasions of Lebanon beginning in 1978, and the Soviet war in Afghanistan all garnered attention and concern in both the West and the Arab world.

On January 15, 1980, *The Guardian* ran a story by Madrid-based journalist Tom Burns reporting as follows:

> The Spanish Prime Minister Mr. Adolfo Suarez spent six hours in Washington yesterday briefing the White House on possible new policy approaches in the Middle East after the Soviet invasion of Afghanistan. The one-day visit, which included meeting with President Carter, Secretary of State Cyrus Vance, and the National Security Adviser, Mr. Zbigniew Brzezinski, was organized last week

after the West German Chancellor, Mr. Helmut Schmidt, met Mr. Suarez while on an official visit here (London). The West German leader was impressed by the possibility of using Spain's contacts with the Arab world, which were cemented by the official visit to Madrid of the Palestinian leader, Mr. Yasser Arafat last fall.

The short article highlighting the delicate dialogues underway caught David's attention. It mentioned the United States, the United Kingdom, the Soviet Union, Spain, West Germany, and the Arab world in just a single paragraph loaded with the underpinnings of diplomacy. Coupled with his classes in the complex history of the Middle East, the multinational participation in the dramas unfolding there suggested an exciting course of study.

The Iran-Iraq War had begun in 1980, just a year and a half after the Iranian Revolution ended the rule of the Shah and brought Khomeini into power. Decades later, in his book *A History of the Middle East Since the Rise of Islam* (2023), David clarified the importance of this power shift, noting that "many coups masquerade as revolutions, but this one was a transfer of power from one class to another and an almost completely altered political system based on a new prevailing ideology—the Islamic Republic of Iran." Dodger teammates had watched with the rest of the Western world as the Shah abandoned his famous gold and silver Peacock Throne in January 1979, fleeing with his empress Farah Pahlavi to Egypt, Morocco, the Bahamas, and finally the United States for cancer treatment. They had followed the resulting seizure of the American embassy in Tehran just two weeks later by Iranian militants and the ensuing hostage crisis. After his medical treatments in the United States, the Shah returned to Egypt, where President Anwar Sadat granted him asylum and where he died the following July. Just a year later Sadat would be dead as well, the victim of assassination in Cairo.

In Iraq, Saddam Hussein had been watching the changes in Iran, wary of the same emerging ideology that David would eventually write about. He was worried about the potential spread of Khomeini's rigid Pan-Islamic doctrines. He also was hopeful that Iraq could replace Iran as the main power player in the Persian Gulf now that the Shah, with his close ties to the West, had been ousted. He saw his moment in 1980 and invaded Iran, a decision that David would explain decades later in *A History of the Middle East Since the Rise of Islam*.

> When Ayatollah Khomeini, the Supreme Guide of the Shiite Islamic Republic of Iran, wanted to export the revolution around the Middle East, Iraq became a natural target. He was fond of saying that he was going to liberate Jerusalem through Baghdad. Saddam thought perhaps the best defense is a good offense; additionally, it was clear that the US was not going to come to the defense of Iran, not after Khomeini's Revolutionary Guards Corps stormed the US embassy in Teheran in 1979 and held 52 US hostages for 444 days.

In 1979 Western news outlets and Arab media covered the invasion differently, presenting diverse views about the harrowing story of violence and war. By the time David took Cantori's class, the conflict was escalating, and other nations were taking sides. The United States, United Kingdom, Soviet Union, France, Italy, and Yugoslavia supported Iraq. Iran's supporters were Syria, Libya, China, North Korea, Israel, Pakistan, and South Yemen. Casualties were high for both Iraqi and Iranian military forces as well as civilians. The *Encyclopedia Britannica* estimates a range from one million to twice that number.

There was an important nonhuman casualty as well: global oil production. When the Syrian government closed its pipeline, which allowed Iraqi oil to reach tankers in the Mediterranean Sea, Iraq's oil revenues were reduced by $5 billion a month. This was an unacceptable predicament for the Western world, which relied on oil from the Middle East to power its energy needs. The United States and Western European countries increased their support for Iraq, providing money and military aid as the war moved toward a dangerous stalemate. As David and his classmates studied these complexities, they could only offer educated guesses about the eventual outcome, something that would not be known for another seven years.

Meanwhile there was trouble in nearby Lebanon. The Palestine Liberation Organization (PLO) had been expelled from Jordan a decade before and had moved its primary operations to Beirut and surrounding areas. By 1981 conflicts had exploded and peacekeeping forces were dispatched from several Arab countries, including Syria. The Arab world watched carefully, and countries examined their old alliances and considered new ones as the turmoil in Lebanon continued into the early 1980s.

The rest of the world was watching too, but Americans also were focused on events closer to home, including a worrisome economic recession. Newly elected President Ronald Reagan promised to lead the country back to prosperity. His easy smile and confidence were comforting as he tackled big domestic issues and navigated international challenges. An unprecedented blizzard in April caused the cancellation of several major league baseball games in the northeast, much to David's dismay. That fall, when the St. Louis Cardinals defeated the Milwaukee Brewers to win their ninth World Series title in September, he cheered, remembering past interactions with the Brewers and their recruiter and coach, KR, during his baseball days. That year also saw the longest lunar eclipse of the twentieth century, the disappointing defeat of the Equal Rights Amendment in Congress, and the first time in history that *Time*'s Man of the Year was a not a human being. The full-color image of a personal computer appeared on the magazine cover instead, announcing the arrival of the information age. David recalled his high school science-fiction essay and smiled, sure that Mr. Canoun was smiling too.

Convinced that the Middle East's importance in world affairs would only increase in the years ahead, David decided to pursue a master's degree in government, political science, or Middle East studies following graduation. He applied to Harvard, Georgetown, University of Chicago, and the Johns Hopkins School of Advanced International Studies. Cantori, now a close friend and mentor, recommended that he enroll in the most difficult senior seminar in the political science department at UMBC in fall 1983, his last semester. He told David that if he did well in that class he was sure to do well in graduate school. Taught by renowned professor and scholar Robert Freedman, the course focused on Soviet foreign policy with a strong emphasis on the USSR's policies in the Middle East.

Freedman completed his undergraduate degree at the University of Pennsylvania and his doctoral degree at Columbia University, where Zbigniew Brzezinski was one of his professors and an important mentor. His unique understanding of the profound divisions in Soviet-dominated Eastern Europe was immensely insightful and an influential component of Freedman's dissertation, "Economic Warfare in the Communist Bloc," which eventually was published as a book in 1972. During the next decades, after Brzezinski moved from the university setting into the bigger world of international affairs, he stayed in touch with Freedman. He served as President Jimmy Carter's national security advisor from 1977 to 1982 during major foreign-policy events, including the Arab oil embargo, the Camp David Accords, the Soviet-Afghan War, the Iranian Revolution, and the Strategic Arms Limitation Talks (SALT) agreements with the Soviet Union.

Western interest in the Soviet Union was already strong when

Freedman joined the faculty of UMBC, and in September 1983, when Russia shot down a Korean airliner that had strayed over Siberia, international attention became even more intense. David registered for Freedman's course, and he approached the professor with questions about the incident just before the fall semester began. Decades later Freedman remembers thinking that David was exceptionally astute to be researching subjects related to the course before it started. The assessment proved true. David earned an A-plus, the only one the professor had ever awarded. Freedman and David formed a bond of respect and friendship that has lasted decades, just as Brzezinski and Freedman had.

David discovered that, like Louis Cantori, Freedman was a fan of the Orioles. In fact, he had played third base and pitched some in his youth and had been a fan of each major league team in the cities where he lived as his career advanced—the Philadelphia Athletics, the Houston Astros, the Milwaukee Brewers, and finally the Orioles. In April 1992 Oriole Park at Camden Yards opened in Baltimore for its first game. The Orioles were enjoying a huge winning streak that season, and according to Freedman it was impossible to get tickets to the games. David's brother, Bob, was working as a banker and had access to a luxury box at the stadium. He had been instructed to invite doctors to fill it in the hopes that they might become customers of the bank. David told Bob he knew a doctor and invited his favorite PhD to one of those early sold-out games. Baseball cemented a bond that has lasted more than forty years, and whenever David is in Baltimore the two friends never miss an Orioles game.

During David's time at UMBC, Freedman organized a conference in Baltimore, inviting ten Middle East scholars, including Louis Cantori, to discuss the conflict escalating in the Arab world since the once-promising Camp David Accords had been signed in

1979. The presentations resulted in a 1984 book, *The Middle East Since Camp David*, edited by Freedman. Cantori outlined how the Egyptian-Israeli peace agreement led to Egypt's ostracism in the Arab world and how the failure to stop Israel's settlements on the West Bank fueled the strong opinion in the Middle East that Egypt had abandoned the Palestinian cause.

Four decades later the Palestinian cause still looms large in the ongoing conflicts in the Middle East. Freedman had hopes that the war that began between Israel and Hamas in 2023 would conclude in 2024, but he tempered his optimism with hard questions. Who is going to rule Gaza? What will the relationship be with the West Bank and Israel? The conundrum reminded him of a pessimistic quip he heard from a British diplomat at a 2024 conference in London:

> An Israeli Jew and a Palestinian Muslim both really want peace between Israel and the Palestinians, but they are frustrated because it just isn't happening. So finally they turn to God and ask, "Is there ever going to be peace between us?" And God thinks for a while and says, "I have good news and bad news." Since both men are optimistic, they want to hear the good news first. And God says, "Yes, there will be peace." They are overjoyed. "So what is the bad news?" they ask. And God says, "Not in my lifetime."

Israeli-Palestinian turmoil made the front page of David's hometown newspaper, the *Baltimore Sun*. On August 2, 1982, its Jerusalem bureau correspondent, G. Jefferson Price III, reported as follows:

> Israel said last night that its fierce bombardment of West Beirut, accompanied by new advances into the city, did not represent a decision to abandon negotiations to remove the Palestinian [*sic*] Liberation Organization from the Lebanese capital. "Don't get

excited," a Foreign Ministry source said yesterday morning as the Israeli army, navy, and air force pummeled Beirut in the most devastating attacks since the beginning of the war in Lebanon eight weeks ago.

More "excitement," in the literal sense of the word, followed when Lebanon's president-elect Bachir Gemayel was assassinated. Most observers concluded that pro-Syrian elements were responsible. The retaliatory massacre of hundreds of Palestinians at the refugee camps of Sabra and Shatila by vengeful Christian Phalangists followed. Some estimates put the death toll as high as two thousand. The United Nations Security Council unanimously demanded a ceasefire. Cantori's and Freedman's students analyzed these events, aware that important and dangerous dramas were taking place on the world stage. As young optimists, they began to consider how they might contribute to possible solutions.

Both the Syrians and the PLO were gaining power in Lebanon, and differing stories emerged about what happened next. Most Western media outlets reported that southern Lebanon had become a convenient launchpad for rocket attacks against Israel, and that of course Israel needed to retaliate. Justin Salhani, writing for Al Jazeera in 2023— just ten days after the shocking terror attack on Israel by Hamas—described that 1982 conflict through a different lens. "Israel invaded Lebanon under the pretense of stopping PLO raids across the border. The Israeli forces, however, progressed as far north as the capital Beirut, laying siege to the largely pro-Palestinian West Beirut." In the same article Hilal Khashan, a professor of political science at the American University of Beirut, explained that the 1982 Israeli invasion helped spark the creation of Hezbollah with the backing of Iran's Islamic Revolutionary Guard Corps (IRGC).

Aftermath of US embassy bombing in Beirut, Lebanon, 1983

In 1983 a car bomb destroyed the US embassy in Beirut and killed more than ninety people, ushering in a new tactic for terrorist groups that would be repeated horrifically in the years ahead. It was followed in October by a bombing of the Marine barracks housed at Beirut International Airport, killing some 240 American soldiers and 58 French military personnel. The attack hastened the removal of the international peacekeeping force that had been sent to oversee the peaceful withdrawal of Yasser Arafat and the PLO and to ensure the safety of the Palestinian civilians who had stayed behind.

While studying these complex tragedies on the world stage, David Lesch tackled more day-to-day aspects of student life. He held various jobs for extra income—as an athletic trainer at a local fitness club, a lifeguard at the pool of a Baltimore apartment complex during the summer, and a records clerk at the army base hospital at Fort Meade, where he worked the graveyard shift while attending classes during the day. At the pool he noticed a statuesque brunette. A recent divorcée, Suzanne Blais worked at the Social Security Administration headquarters. Romance was back in David's life.

Like Cara, Suzanne was impressed by David's maturity. He was worried that he did not seem to have much going for him as a former baseball player attending a somewhat mediocre college and working as a lifeguard at an apartment complex, but she saw more. She praised his intelligence and kindness, and she was absolutely convinced that his prospects for the future were bright, regardless of what he chose as his next career. For David, still recovering from a volatile breakup with Lisa, this was a welcome change. Suzanne seemed to offer a stable, mature presence in his life.

That future took a life-changing turn in the summer of 1984 with an opportunity to experience the Arab world firsthand. He was chosen to join a small group of graduating seniors from around the country, led by Louis Cantori, to study in Egypt for nearly three months. Funded by the Fulbright Commissions, the program introduced the students to the history, culture, language, economics, and country's political landscape. They toured the major Islamic sites in Cairo, rode camels around the Pyramids of Giza, visited Luxor and Abu Simbel, climbed Mount Sinai (Jabal Musa), and went snorkeling at Ras Muhammad at the southern tip of the Sinai Peninsula. They also explored popular places, far from the important religious and historic sites.

Cantori took them to a section of the city inhabited by "People of the Trash," where extremely poor people lived in little shacks built of rubbish and discarded boxes. The open sewage created a terrible stench. David wrote in his journal that "we had to cover our noses with handkerchiefs; this was poverty beyond anything we had ever seen in the United States. Yet some of the inhabitants came out of their makeshift homes to offer food to the group—probably a month's worth of food for them." He was astounded by the Arab culture's deep commitment to hospitality, something he would experience repeatedly in the years ahead.

Cairo was a dense and overcrowded city. Its souks (markets) created labyrinths of tented alleyways where stalls with everything from fragrant spices to handwoven carpets and silver jewelry delighted the senses. David loved getting lost in the huge Khan al-Khalili souk, an adventure he would repeat in every Middle Eastern country he would eventually visit. He learned to navigate streets with heavy traffic, realizing that a flick of headlights indicated an approaching car's invitation to cross, and to keep a careful eye out for pickpockets in the crowds. When Cantori, who had spent so much time in Cairo, had his wallet stolen near the souk, he simply smiled and told the students that he admired the expertise of the thief and that the crime really was an art form in Cairo.

When he returned from Egypt, David learned that his applications to graduate school had all received acceptances. All except Harvard offered him a full scholarship, but he chose it anyway, grateful for the Dodgers' continuing contribution toward his tuition. He had felt a twinge of doubt when he applied to the prestigious university, aware that his grades weren't the best in his class and that the University of Maryland was not an established pathway to Ivy League graduate school. But an early lesson from his pitching days, when he faced some of the most challenging batters without fear of failure, had become rooted in his psyche. "Never eliminate yourself" was a resounding inner command that he followed when he dared to apply to universities that might have seemed out of reach. He learned later from a professor on Harvard's selection committee that his baseball background had made his application different and interesting and that his obvious resilience and perseverance had been key assets. He would need those for the stresses of graduate school and beyond.

Harvard's Center for Middle Eastern Studies was located not far from the school's Museum of the Ancient Near East, a red brick repository built in 1889, more than two hundred years after the university was founded in 1636. Harvard was early in recognizing the importance of that faraway region. Its pursuit of firsthand knowledge about the Middle East, based on literacy in its languages and understanding of its diverse politics, cultures, and histories, spans centuries. Distinguished alumni of the center have followed careers in government, academia, business, journalism, and law, and many are well-known leaders working globally today.

David walked up the steps to the center's front porch on a brisk September day in 1984. He took a breath of cool Boston air and exhaled slowly. A new chapter was beginning. The study load was intense, but as always, he found time for sports—organizing, coaching, and leading a team appropriately named the Shaykhs in the graduate school intramural basketball league. They made it to the championship game both years he was at the center but were beaten both times by the Harvard Business School team, which had a much larger pool of talent from which to draw. The center's director, Nadav Safran, was a regular spectator at the games. Whenever the Shaykhs won he would light a cigar, emulating the famous coach of the Boston Celtics, Red Auerbach.

Safran was born in Egypt, moved to a kibbutz when he was twenty-one, and fought as a lieutenant in the 1948 Arab-Israeli War. After the armistice was signed, he moved to the United States, where he earned an undergraduate degree at Brandeis University and a doctoral degree at Harvard, studying under Henry Kissinger. He later taught government and worked as a

The Shaykhs (from left): Kurt Opperman, Martin Ingall, David Lesch, Ken Greenwald, Rob Satloff, Chris Brown, and Professor Nadav Safran

research fellow before becoming director of the center. Known as a tough professor, Safran did not hesitate to extoll his students when they did well or to embarrass them when they did not. He threw one young man's final paper across the room in disgust, shouting that it was poorly done and that his oral presentation was even worse. David was more fortunate. He received a high A in Safran's seminar on the Persian Gulf and gained a mentor who began to encourage him to think about applying for the doctoral program in Harvard's Department of Government.

During the Christmas break in 1984, David stayed at Suzanne's condo in Columbia, Maryland. On Christmas Eve, while sitting under the Christmas tree, he asked her to marry him. Instead of going down on one knee, he got up on one knee to propose. Her response was an immediate yes and she fell back on the floor when she saw the ring he had purchased, cleverly set to look bigger than it was. She was thrilled. They talked about getting married within the next year. One of the most harrowing events of David's life would delay the wedding until June 1986, however, just after he received his master's degree in Middle Eastern studies.

The new year began happily despite the record cold in Cambridge, where the high temperature was only twelve degrees on January 21. The campus was blanketed in snow, a lovely sight from the center's third-floor windows. As David watched the accumulation of soft flakes below, he savored his memories of the recent holidays spent in Baltimore with his parents, brother Bob, and fiancée Suzanne. The future felt especially promising. Safran was championing his dreams of earning a doctorate from Harvard, and his engagement to Suzanne was official.

The semester flew by. Safran had insisted that David take courses in the government department from several legendary Harvard professors—Joseph Nye, Robert Keohane, and Samuel Huntington. All had received their doctorates from Harvard, had written important books in the field of international relations, and would go on to serve in various capacities in government. Nye and Keohane were cofounders of the theory of neoliberalism and coauthors of the 1977 book *Power and Interdependence*, and Keohane was the Stanfield Professor of International Peace at Harvard. Nye was serving as director of the Center for Science and International Affairs when David enrolled in his course, and he would eventually become the assistant secretary of defense for international security affairs during Bill Clinton's presidency.

Huntington had earned his doctoral degree at Harvard and began teaching there when he was only twenty-three. Along with his colleague Zbigniew Brzezinski, he was denied tenure in 1959 and moved to Columbia University. He was invited to return to Harvard with tenure in 1963, and when Brzezinski was appointed national security advisor by President Jimmy Carter in 1977, he was selected as the White House coordinator of security planning for the National Security Council. When David took his class at Harvard in 1985, he was introduced to Huntington's developing theory that future wars would be fought not between countries but between cultures and that Islamic civilization would become the biggest threat to Western domination of the world.

Events unfolding in the Arab countries in the 1980s seemed to support Huntington's theory. Since the start of the conflict between the Arab states and the State of Israel, Lebanon found itself squeezed between Israel and Syria, its combative larger neighbors. President Hafez al-Assad told the *New York Times*, "Lebanon and Syria are one single people, one single nation. We may be divided into two independent states, but that does not mean that we are two different nations....I would even argue that the feeling of kinship between Syria and Lebanon runs deeper than it does between states in the United States."

As a result of exhilarating discussions with his professors, hours spent in the library, and expanded news coverage of international events, David's thoughts about pursuing a doctorate in government or foreign affairs grew more serious. Television experienced a revolution when media mogul Ted Turner established the Cable News Network (CNN), the world's first twenty-four-hour news network, in 1980. Suddenly audiences could see on-the-spot images and hear diverse voices from anywhere on the planet. They saw the aftermath of John Lennon's assassination outside his apartment in New York; they witnessed President Reagan get shot by John Hinkley Jr. as he left the Washington Hilton in 1981; they watched in horror as NASA's Space Shuttle *Challenger* exploded shortly after takeoff in 1986. At the end of the decade they celebrated the fall of the Berlin Wall, cheering along with the crowds of East Germans tearing down the symbol of the Cold War. And, of course, images of bombings and devastation in the Middle East poured into living rooms across America, as they still do today.

CNN also covered a horrific event in David's hometown that profoundly affected his life and the plans he had made. In early July 1985 David's parents ran over something as they were driving home from a dinner party. They heard a loud clunk as the object hit the bottom of their 1978 Buick Regal sedan. The next day they took the car to the Chevron gas station they always used. There was a hole in the gas tank, which was repaired, or so they thought. The gas tank began leaking the night of July 16, and when Warren and Margaret awakened the next morning, they smelled gasoline permeating the house. They followed the smell to the basement and entered the garage. Warren knew he had to open the garage door to let the gas fumes out. But when he pushed the button of the automatic door opener, the light went on and everything exploded. Somehow they made it back to the basement, up the stairs to the living room, and out the front door before collapsing on the front lawn. Neighbors came running to help. A medivac helicopter landed in the street and took them to Francis Scott Key Medical Center in Baltimore.

David's childhood friend, Doug Reitz, saw the huge plumes of black smoke from his house around the block. He drove over immediately, and flames were everywhere. "It is one of my most horrific memories," he recalls forty years later, "and I know the impact on David and Bob was immense. Their world had quite literally blown up." Margaret was burned over more than 75 percent of her body, and 66 percent of Warren's body was burned. Fortunately their faces were relatively unscathed. Miraculously they both had turned away from the blast in time. It was also fortuitous that the hospital had one of the finest burn units in the country, which no doubt saved their lives.

CURVEBALLS

Bob had recently moved into a condominium he called his bachelor pad about twenty minutes away. David was living with Suzanne in her condominium about an hour away. The next-door neighbor, Wayne Kasecamp, called both brothers and they raced to the hospital, unsure if they would find their parents alive. The doctors took them to see their mother immediately because she was not expected to live. As a devout Catholic, she already had been given last rites.

What they saw in the hospital room was unimaginably grue-some—the charred and bloated body of the mother they adored, a vision that was forever imprinted in their memories. Both David and Bob became nauseous and could barely stand. Despite her condition, she was able to speak to her boys. She asked them if they were okay, and she told them it was important for them to cry, that she knew they had lost so much in the fire. She told them she loved them as the doctors rolled her back to the operat-ing room to try to save her life.

To this day David is emotional when he remembers that July day in 1985. Despite his mother's unbelievable pain, she was most worried about her boys. He calls it "supreme empathy and love." In the years ahead, pursuing what would become his career, he would meet many people in the Middle East who had lost their homes and loved ones to blasts and fires in multiple wars. When he told them that he felt their pain and loss, cried with them, prayed with them, and worked to help find peaceful solutions amid chaos and violence, they could sense his authenticity and empathy. They knew he had felt the same emotions they were experiencing, although at another time and place in the world.

That place was the state-of-the-art hospital in Baltimore, where Warren had been upgraded from critical to serious condi-tion and Margaret was fighting for her life. David and Bob tried to reassure their father that their mother was a fighter with strong

Couple burned seriously in fire from gas fumes

By Barbara Taylor

A garage filled with gasoline vapor exploded into a fireball yesterday morning in Bel Air's Glenwood development, leaving a doctor and his wife critically burned and destroying their home, fire officials said.

Dr. Warren Lesch, 56, and his wife, Margaret, 53, were flown by State Police helicopter to the Francis Scott Key Burn Center after the 7 a.m. fire in the 400 block Glenwood road, reports said.

Both Dr. and Mrs. Lesch have second- and third-degree burns, a hospital spokeswoman said.

The home, valued at $200,000, was destroyed. "We're looking at a foundation now," Bob Thomas, a spokesman for the state fire marshal, said.

The fire began when Dr. Lesch, a general practitioner, and his wife went to investigate the gasoline fumes that had seeped into their one-story, wood-frame home. Their car had leaked gas through the night and flipping on an electric garage door-opener was enough to ignite the fumes, Mr. Thomas said.

"It exploded into a fireball and, in 15 minutes, it was gone," he said.

Mr. Thomas said about 50 firefighters from four departments battled the fire for almost an hour. The fire threw debris up to 30 yards, but was confined to the Lesch home. One fireman sprained his ankle and cut his leg.

The explosion rocked homes up

See **FIRE**, 2F, Col. 5

Only rubble remains after fire at doctor's home in Bel Air.

Story of the Lesch house fire in the *Baltimore Sun*, July 18, 1985

faith and that she would pull through. She did, but the next few weeks were a seemingly endless nightmare. The debridement treatments to remove her charred skin were terribly painful, and her screams were something Warren and her sons could never forget.

As both parents began their slow recovery, David and Bob were dealing with the remains of their family home. Everything had burned—furniture, artwork, dishes and silverware, clothing, and of course the structure itself. Only one item survived and was found in the charred ruins: David's Dodgers championship ring from the Lethbridge team in the Pioneer League. Mostly unscathed, it had a tiny burn mark on one side. It remains a lifelong reminder of two very important but tremendously different moments in David's life.

Margaret and Warren required special care, including delicate skin grafts, for months. Eventually they moved from the hospital into Bob's townhouse, no longer a bachelor pad, while they rebuilt their house on its original site. It was a duplicate, with a few modern updates, of the house that had been destroyed. A year and a half after the accident they moved back to 404 Glenwood Road.

The months took a toll on David. In addition to the emotional experience of nearly losing his parents, there were legal and administrative chores resulting from the fire and architectural and construction decisions to be made as the Lesch family's new home literally rose like a phoenix from the ashes. His grades slipped during the fall semester, and an extraordinary scandal engulfed his biggest advocate at Harvard, Nadav Safran. David realized that a doctorate in government probably was not in the cards. But as he had done before when faced with a roadblock, he found another path.

The *Boston Globe* cover story about Nadav Safran's CIA funding, October 11, 1985

FINDING HOME BASE

On October 11, 1985, both the *Boston Globe* and the *Harvard Crimson* carried the explosive news that the director of Harvard's Center for Middle Eastern Studies had accepted more than $150,000 from the US Central Intelligence Agency (CIA) without informing the university. Nadav Safran claimed to have used $107,430 to help support his writing of *Saudi Arabia: The Ceaseless Quest for Security*, which had been published by Harvard University Press earlier that year. In the book's preface the Rockefeller Foundation and the Rand Corporation were acknowledged as funding sources, but the CIA was not.

Safran had also accepted $50,000 from the CIA for a closed conference on Islam and Muslim politics, scheduled to take place at the Faculty Club just a week after the story broke. More than ninety prominent Middle East scholars from around the world were registered to attend, and David was looking forward to participating in the conference and to the exhilarating discussions with his mentor that would surely follow. He knew the proceedings would be off the record and closed to the public and the press, but Safran had told him the results would eventually be published.

The conference participants would have lots to discuss. On October 1, 1985, Israel launched Operation Wooden Leg, an airstrike on the PLO's headquarters in Tunisia, established after being driven out of Lebanon in 1982. With a destination more than fifteen hundred miles away, ten Israeli F-15 fighter jets flew toward Tunis, refueling over the Mediterranean Sea thanks to two Boeing 707 tankers. They launched precision-guided munitions to destroy the sand-colored buildings along the coast that had been the PLO's stronghold for three years. The attack lasted only six minutes. The site was obliterated, and reports of casualties ranged from forty-seven to sixty dead and sixty-five to one hundred wounded. Because the attack occurred so far from Israel, Tunisia's president suggested that there might have been American collaboration.

Israel claimed that the airstrike was in retaliation for a complex plan by the PLO to attack Israel's military headquarters in Tel Aviv six months earlier. The plot had called for the use of freighters to carry PLO fighters across the Mediterranean, a transfer to rubber dinghies to carry them to shore, and the hijacking of several buses to force the drivers to take them to Tel Aviv. Once there, they planned to storm the compound, kill as many people as they could, and take hostages who could be exchanged for Palestinian prisoners held in Israeli jails. But Israel's intelligence agency, Mossad, discovered the plot in April. The freighters transporting PLO fighters were sunk by Israeli missile boats, and Israel's defense minister Yitzhak Rabin ordered plans drawn up for a retaliatory strike. When Operation Wooden Leg destroyed the PLO headquarters in October, Prime Minister Shimon Peres said, "It was an act of self-defense. Period."

At first the US government voiced support for Israel's actions in 1985, but as the international backlash increased, the United Nations Security Council condemned the attack as a flagrant

FINDING HOME BASE

violation of the UN Charter. President Reagan joined the majority of world leaders expressing criticism. In the days preceding the planned conference at Harvard, news outlets covered this latest upheaval in the Middle East.

The *Boston Globe* also picked up the story involving Safran, the CIA, and Harvard's Center for Middle Eastern Studies. Safran told the *Globe* that there were "gross distortions" in the *Crimson* article, but the scandal escalated. Over the next few weeks scrutiny of David's controversial mentor increased. Questions about funding for an earlier conference on the Persian Gulf emerged. Safran would not disclose where money for that conference came from, and the CIA refused to comment about any of the grants. Several former directors of the Center for Middle Eastern Studies were adamant that funding from the CIA, Middle Eastern governments, and "other interested parties" was never acceptable. Safran stepped down as the center's director but retained his position on the university faculty.

One of Harvard's most respected professors was suddenly no longer the champion David had counted on as he prepared his applications for graduate school. Pivoting to other options, he switched his goal to a doctorate in history, a field that had captivated his interest thanks to professors like Freedman and Cantori, who were happy to supply glowing recommendations to the admissions office. The following summer, with his master's degree in hand, he married Suzanne in a Catholic ceremony in downtown Baltimore. His parents had recovered sufficiently from the fire to attend the wedding and reception, and it was their first outing in almost a year. David had been accepted to the doctoral program at Harvard and had chosen to write his dissertation on US-Syria relations. As everyone celebrated on that June afternoon, they toasted 1986 as a year of important new beginnings.

His interest in Syria was not new. It had been building for the last few years, fueled by scholars like Patrick Seale, whose 1965 book *The Struggle for Syria* was required reading for anyone interested in the country's modern history. It made the case that Syria was the keystone in the international power games that had occurred in the Middle East in the 1950s and 1960s. When David's dissertation adviser, Philip Khoury, told him the historian was scheduled to speak at the Massachusetts Institute of Technology nearby, David attended. The presentation was riveting, and a one-on-one conversation followed. Seale expressed excitement about David's dissertation, especially when he shared that recently declassified documents would add a new perspective to the topic that fascinated them both. A lifelong friendship began. In 1988 Seale wrote *Asad: The Struggle for the Middle East*, the definitive biography of Hafez al-Assad, who ruled Syria as its president from 1971 until his death in 2000. David, of course, later wrote about al-Assad's son Bashar and documented his rise to power in *The New Lion of Damascus*.

But David's connection to Syria was still in its infancy when he returned to Harvard in the fall of 1986. He and Suzanne rented an apartment in Cambridge, close to campus. Suzanne transferred from the Social Security Administration headquarters to its office in Boston, providing much-needed income and resigning herself to a terrible commute via bus and two subway line transfers. In addition to carrying a demanding course load, David worked as a teaching assistant for two professors. One was his mentor Nadav Safran, whose teaching style and rumored ties to the CIA made him immensely popular with his students. Harvard professors typically taught their classes of thirty to forty students in a lecture format, counting on three teaching assistants (TAs) to work with ten or so students in seminar settings, inviting questions and discussion and providing individual help when needed. TA positions were highly sought after, and they paid well. To be considered, a graduate student first had to excel in the professor's class and, once chosen as a TA, undergo regular performance evaluations. While some Harvard graduate students feared those intense evaluations, David embraced them. They reminded him of the coaching he had valued so much in the sports world. He understood that to get better at anything, constructive criticism was essential.

Tom Ewald was one of the Harvard undergraduates David taught. His father, William Ewald Jr., had worked at the White House as a speechwriter for President Dwight Eisenhower as a young man and had served as assistant to the secretary of the interior in the late 1950s. He became a senior executive at IBM and eventually cowrote Eisenhower's presidential memoirs with John Eisenhower, which were published in 1992. Ewald's mother was a civic leader and poet. Both parents had earned doctoral degrees at Harvard and worked there as professors. They prized education and exposed their children to travel and cultural diversity at an early age. When Tom was in the fifth grade, the family explored Spain and Morocco. In the decades that followed his adventures grew more daring, eventually including a brief stay in a Pakistani prison and a harrowing experience as a hostage in Iraq.

While at Harvard, majoring in English literature, he chose a course in contemporary Middle East politics to satisfy a required elective. He remembers that the professor was quite respected and had just written a book. But the two-hour lectures consisted of him simply reading long passages from it. "He was truly awful," Ewald says, forty years later. "I felt like clunking my head on the desk." Fortunately there was a seminar for the class, and David Lesch was teaching it.

I still remember the first day of that seminar. David talked about the Iran-Iraq War and asked which country Syria had supported during the conflict. He reminded us that the president of Iraq was Saddam Hussein, and the president of Syria was Hafez al-Assad, and that while both were members of the Ba'ath Socialist Party, they were bitter rivals. After giving us that hint, he waited for someone to raise his hand. Finally someone did and gave his answer—Iraq. I could not believe it! David was not surprised or upset. He told me later that he understood not everyone was interested in the subject, that sometimes an unexpected catalyst was needed, and he shared his own unusual journey from a career in baseball to a PhD candidate at Harvard. I think there was a secret sauce to David's special teaching style—he was humble about his past; he was not judgmental, and he was kind. He simply hoped his students would come around by the end of the seminar—and they did.

Another ingredient in that formula was David's addition of fascinating glimpses into important behind-the-scenes moments in history, like the secret meetings that took place between Saddam Hussein and Hafez al-Assad in 1987. Saddam famously announced that "there will be no handshakes and no greetings because we are at odds," and Hafez reportedly laughed at how the Iraqi leader began the meeting "in such a tense and tactless manner."

After graduating summa cum laude from Harvard, Ewald was hired by Barclays, but his interest in the Middle East continued to simmer and an unexpected opportunity catapulted him into an unforgettable adventure. When Al Ahli Bank of Kuwait offered him the position of deputy head of international lending, he was thrilled. He arrived in Kuwait City on July 30, 1990, a day when the temperature set a new record at 116 degrees. Just three days later Kuwait became another sort of hotspot. On August 2

Longtime adversaries Saddam Hussein and Hafez al-Assad, 1987

Iraq invaded the small pro-West country, and twenty-five-year-old Ewald was one of hundreds of Americans and other nationalities taken hostage.

Some incredible developments followed. He was the first hostage to be released, after only six weeks of captivity in Iraq. His mother, Mary Ewald, was at the heart of the unusual story that captivated readers around the world. Immediately after hearing that her son had been taken hostage, she and her husband went to the Iraqi embassy in Washington and knocked on the door. No one else was knocking on that door since the ambassador already had returned to Iraq and negative media attention had erupted. Protestors lined the embassy's courtyard. But the chargé d'affaires was still there. During their meeting, Mary discovered he had studied English literature in the United States and shared her love for the poems of Geoffrey Chaucer. The Ewalds described their extensive travels and their respect for Muslims and Islam, and Mary asked if she could write a letter to Saddam Hussein and if the chargé d'affaires would guarantee its delivery. Miraculously

Hussein received the letter and released Ewald to American embassy officials in Baghdad. He was sent to London on a chartered Air Iraq plane just six weeks after the invasion. The letter Mary wrote to Iraq's president became an example of persuasive writing that is studied in English classes today. It is also a testimony to the importance of finding common ground, reflecting international diplomacy at its best.

Ewald immediately telephoned his parents from his London hotel room, and as he looked through the one small suitcase that had traveled from Kuwait to Iraq to the UK, he spotted a business card lodged in the bottom. It was David's. He was sure that his friend and former teacher was aware he'd been taken hostage and knew he must be worried. As Ewald recounts, "I called him and said, 'David, it's Tom.' There was a long pause. This was not the reaction I was expecting from the teacher who inspired me to go to the Middle East. I added, 'Tom Ewald.' There was another pause, then he asked how things were going. I told him I had been released, and there was another pause. 'From where?' he asked."

Of course, David quickly realized the importance of the call and the excitement that would follow when Ewald returned to the United States a few days later. When the plane landed in Baltimore, Tom's family, a military band, and lots of media created a hero's welcome. David was there as well, greeting him and thanking him for the call from London, with firsthand information that made David a popular commentator for television news outlets looking for insights about the situation in the Middle East.

David's next taste of international life was not quite as dramatic as Ewald's. It was not life threatening, but it was life changing. In 1988 he was awarded a special travel fellowship by the Boston-based Marion and Jaspar Whiting Foundation. Recipients of these competitive scholarships received funding to

The Public Record Office in London, repository of the U.K. national archives until 2003

study abroad in countries that would expose them to a variety of worldviews and enhance their future teaching abilities. When he won the fellowship, David knew he had hit a home run. He would be away for six months studying in London, Paris, and the country that had been calling to him: Syria. Suzanne did not accompany him, realizing that his studies would be totally absorbing, and she was happy to return to the Baltimore area to resume her job at the Social Security headquarters. Together they decided that sometime during his sojourn in Europe she and her mother would visit.

When David arrived in London in January 1989, sunshine and warmth welcomed him. He was happily surprised as everyone had told him that London weather was always cold and rainy. The next day he realized that everyone was right. The sun did not shine again during his stay. Maryland House was home for the next sixty days, and he smiled at the coincidence of its name and wondered if it was a sign of good luck. Located in Russell Square in central London, it provided inexpensive lodging for graduate students and, of course, looked nothing like student housing across the Atlantic. A bit dilapidated, with sporadic heat and an unusual bathroom where the showerhead was installed in the ceiling, it was not the cozy room with a fireplace so often depicted in novels. He ate his first British dinner at the cafeteria in Maryland House. To his surprise, the special that night was "Maryland fried chicken."

His days were spent in the Public Records Office, the British equivalent of the National Archives in the United States. Located in Kew Gardens, the office was a forty-five-minute journey on the Tube, London's subway system. Inside Public Records he discovered a treasure trove of information. The files were far more revealing than those he had accessed in the United States at the National Archives in Washington, the Eisenhower Presidential

Library in Kansas, the John Foster Dulles Collection at Princeton University, and the Truman Presidential Library in Missouri. Delving into the British archives from the 1950s was as enlightening as he had imagined. They described meetings about events in Syria that had been attended by representatives of various countries, and the transcripts had been filed without the redactions that they had undergone in the United States. Names, locations, and ideas were not blacked out and the information was astounding. By triangulating his sources, using archives in the United States, the UK, and France, David knew he could piece together a more thorough history of the Middle East that would make his dissertation—and the book that followed—particularly important in the years ahead.

While research and writing dominated the eight weeks he spent in London, David found time to explore the city on the weekends. Walking was his favorite mode of transportation. He could discover both the city's well-known landmarks and the hidden corners. He met other scholars at Public Records. All were on a budget, and they often visited inexpensive cafés and pubs together, where they had a few pints, dined on fish and chips, and discussed the history of the Middle East, international challenges, and ideas for peaceful solutions. Most went on to join universities as faculty, international think tanks, and government agencies.

Robert Satloff, already a friend from Harvard and a teammate from the Shaykhs, was working on his dissertation at Oxford University and spending a lot of time at Public Records. He would soon start a long career with the Washington Institute for Near East Policy, founded in 1985 by veteran diplomat and former US ambassador to Israel Martin Indyk; Satloff became executive director in 1993. David also met Paul Kingston, another doctoral candidate at Oxford, who would go on to become a professor at the University of Toronto. Kingston contributed a chapter to one of David's later books. Lifelong friendships were made. To this day, on his frequent visits to London, whenever David walks past a fish and chips joint, fond memories of those student days come flooding back, along with not-so-fond recollections of his daily cuisine.

His wife, Suzanne, and her mother, Maxine, arrived a week before David's London studies ended. Since he had walked through every borough of the historic city, he knew it well. He took them on a whirlwind tour, including Buckingham Palace, the Tower of London, Westminster Abbey, the British Museum, and a special visit to the Churchill War Rooms, and they splurged on a few nights in a hotel.

Paris was the next destination for David's triangulated research project. Suzanne and her mother accompanied him, spending another week in Europe and exploring the City of Light. They crossed the English Channel on the hydrofoil and took the train to Paris, where David had arranged for an inexpensive apartment in the Latin Quarter near the Sorbonne on the Left Bank. After a week of sightseeing, Suzanne and her mother returned to Maryland, and David immersed himself in research at the Ministry of Foreign Affairs. In contrast to the British, the French had not declassified as much information from the 1950s, but the next few weeks yielded a few important new facts. The French had a long history in Syria, having been the supervisory mandate power there from the 1920s to the early 1940s between the two world wars. As such, the archives had more interesting and detailed information on prominent Syrian politicians from those days who remained influential in Syria in the 1950s.

David again explored the city on foot, absorbing its colors, noises, smells, and culture. There were no other scholars to interact with at the ministry, so walking provided his interaction with people and places. He grew to love this method of discovery, never dreaming that it would play an important role in his work in the Middle East.

At last it was time for the final segment of the Whiting fellowship. David could hardly contain his excitement to experience the country he had been studying for so long. In 1989 Syria was very closed off. Not many Americans had visited, and David realized he was entering little-known territory. He had carefully scheduled interviews with retired Syrian diplomats who had been active in the 1950s and could comment directly on historical events described in his dissertation. But shortly before he arrived, the interviews were canceled, reflective of Syria's growing displeasure with the United States over accusations about possible Syrian involvement in the bombing of Pan Am Flight 103 over Lockerbie, Scotland, on December 21, 1988.

After landing in Damascus, David was directed to the back of the line to clear customs, indicative of a less than warm welcome for an arriving American. He watched as several hundred Iranian women in full chadors were greeted with smiles and ushered to the front of the line. His wait lasted more than an hour. Exhausted, he made his way to the least expensive hotel he could find, booked sight unseen from Paris. Located in Martyrs' Square, in the old part of the city, it turned out to be a favorite accommodation for Iranian Shia pilgrims. A large portrait of the Ayatollah Khomeini, Iran's supreme leader, dominated the entrance to the hotel's shabby lobby. Syria and Iran had been allies since 1980, when the Iran-Iraq War began. As David had told his students at Harvard, Hafez al-Assad and Saddam Hussein were bitter rivals, and it was a given that Syria would side with Iran in the war. It was also a given that Iranian pilgrims would feel welcome in Syria, where ancient Shiite shrines were numerous.

As he had done in London and Paris, David explored much of

Syrian port city of Tartus on the Mediterranean coast

Damascus on foot. Since his interviews with retired Syrian diplomats had been canceled, he devised a new plan to learn about the country. He traveled on local buses, practicing his Arabic with fellow passengers and immersing himself in the culture. He visited historic sites and discovered the hospitality of the Syrian people. Remembering his experiences in Egypt in 1984, he was not surprised by their custom of offering food or drink to any visitor, sometimes when they had little to spare. He witnessed firsthand the Islamic edict to treat others well, no matter their race, religion, or nationality.

A visit to the port city of Tartus provided an experience that proved that edict in a personal way. Located not far from Syria's border with Lebanon, Tartus was a Phoenician colony during the second millennium BCE. Emperor Constantine I rebuilt it in 346 CE, and it flourished during Roman and Byzantine times. It became an important trade center during the Ottoman Empire. In 1989 it was a vacation spot for Syrians, with a beautiful sea corniche (coastal road) overlooking a soft sand beach and the Mediterranean Sea. A meeting on that corniche sealed his love for the country and its people. Two soldiers, on leave from the Syrian army, realized that David was not a local and approached him. They told him they were cousins and, fascinated to learn he was from the United States, began to pepper him with questions about the country they had heard so much about. After a long walk along the beach, they invited David to join them at their home for dinner that night. He accepted with alacrity.

When his new friends took him to their home, the entire extended family was there to greet him. They formed two columns in front of what was not much more than a shack and invited David to walk through. When he did, they began to clap and sing songs of welcome. It was crowded inside, packed with the soldiers' parents, grandparents, aunts, uncles, and cousins. They had put together a feast far beyond their economic circumstances. David shared stories in his less-than-perfect Arabic. A few of the hosts tested their English, and the grandparents still remembered some French from the days when it was the country's second language. It was an unforgettable night, and the next morning the new friends met at the corniche to say goodbye. The young Syrian soldiers started crying. Everyone hugged and kissed, and David would never forget the generosity he experienced that night.

After nearly two months of traveling all over Syria, in May 1989 he visited Latakia, on the country's upper northwest coast, on the Mediterranean. Famous for its beaches and water sports, it is popular as a vacation city, and the Assad family long had a large compound there. It was also a known port of call for the Soviet navy. On his last night in town, David stopped at a café adjacent to the port where some Russian sailors were drinking vodka. They invited him to join them, and despite the language barrier, they enjoyed a grand time that ended with drunken songs and hugs of friendship. Early the next morning David was awakened by loud explosions that rocked him out of bed and shattered his hotel room window. Fearing the worst, he peered out of the window and saw that the Soviet cruiser was on fire. It had either been attacked or something on the ship had exploded. He decided that if it had been attacked, it was either by Israel or the United States. His best option was to leave Syria immediately by crossing the nearby border into Turkey.

Fortunately he had cash. Because Syria did not have ATMs or accept credit cards, he had sold most of his clothes before traveling to Latakia so he would have enough money for his seaside adventure. He took a quick shower before going to the lobby to check out. He noticed that the water circling the drain was dark brown and knelt down to investigate, though he could not see well without his glasses. He discovered thousands of ants swarming the shower floor. When the desk clerk presented a bill that was higher than quoted, he mustered his best Arabic and yelled that his stay had been terrible—explosions across the street, a shattered window, and ants in the shower. The clerk agreed to the original price and David hired a taxi to drive him the short distance to the Turkish border.

As he approached the border facility to get his passport stamped and obtain a visa to enter Turkey, two busloads of Iranian women in full chadors pulled up to the building. Certain that he would again be directed to the end of the line with the same long wait he had endured in Damascus, he groaned with frustration. One of the Turkish guards saw immediately that he was American, and he was escorted to the commandant's office. Visions of the horrific Turkish prison in the film *Midnight Express* flashed through his head as he wondered what was next. But the commandant could not have been nicer. He offered

David tea, discussed American movies, stamped his documents, and expedited his departure by instructing the guards to push past the line of Iranians waiting to cross the border. The tables had turned. Entering Syria, he had seen Iranians receive preferential treatment in the immigration line; entering Turkey as an American, it was his turn to move speedily through the process.

David waved a thank you to the commandant and hired a taxi to drive twelve miles to Antakya. Known in ancient times as Antioch, it had been the capital of the province of Syria during the Roman Empire and was now a town in south-central Turkey. Perched high above the Orontes River, for about six centuries it had dominated the Eastern Mediterranean. Its cosmopolitan population comprised of Greeks, Macedonians, Jews, Phoenicians, Armenians, Syrians, and Romans made it one of the world's most diverse cities. All free men, irrespective of origin, held equal citizenship status. David considered this noble concept, which was certainly missing in the modern world of the Middle East and beyond.

He was back in a place where credit cards were accepted, so he bought new clothes and withdrew more cash. A few days later an article in the international edition of *USA Today* revealed the cause of the explosion in Latakia. Two Syrian helicopter gunships had attacked the Soviet cruiser. At least two sailors were killed, potentially the men he had been drinking with the night before. The Syrian government called it a tragic misunderstanding. There was speculation that it was a not-so-subtle message from Syrian president Hafez al-Assad to Soviet president Mikhail Gorbachev that he did not like recent indications that the Soviet-US relationship was warming, a hint that the Cold War might be thawing.

After a breakfast of *tava boregi*—pastries that surpass the ultimate sensation of sweet—and the strong coffee Turkey is famous for, David was well fortified for a tour of the town. With its proximity to Jerusalem, Antioch in the first century CE became the "cradle of Christianity" and home of the world's first Christian community. David visited the Church of Saint Peter, one of Christianity's oldest churches in a mountainside cave, saw the remains of the ancient Roman aqueduct, and hiked to the rock arches and ruins of rock tombs that had been cut into the surrounding mountains thousands of years earlier. He traveled through historic towns along the Turquoise Coast, including Alanya, Antalya, and Bodrum, and finally arrived in Istanbul for his flight back to the United States.

By the time he returned to Baltimore, he had fallen in love with Syria and its people. He told his friends and family that he was sure about his career choice as a historian and his focus on the Middle East. He felt the same confidence that had once empowered him on the baseball diamond. Over the next decades he would teach more than four thousand students, publish eighteen books, and visit Syria more than thirty times, becoming one of the most knowledgeable professors of Middle Eastern studies. He would also incorporate his love of walking, honed to new levels during his travels, into his future work in conflict resolution, based on understanding other cultures and finding common ground.

But first, in late 1990, he completed the final research for his dissertation, using thousands of documents he had gathered, most in English and some in French and Arabic, from the dozens of archives he had visited in the United States and abroad. He did most of his writing in the condominium he and Suzanne shared in Columbia, Maryland, a short drive away from research resources in Washington. He also taught a course at UMBC and another at Johns Hopkins University and worked as a commentator for a local news television station to supplement his

FINDING HOME BASE 77

income. His interview with Tom Ewald following the Kuwait hostage crisis attracted a huge viewership. A bit of a jokester, Ewald laughingly credits something other than the riveting story for the big market share. "David was so easy on the eyes. The producer knew how to boost the audience of women between eighteen and sixty," he says.

But as the new decade began, David knew that stories about conflicts in the Middle East would continue to attract big audiences for reasons that had nothing to do with the messengers' physical appearances. He was right. Today diplomats and scholars describe the Iraqi invasion of Kuwait as the "beginning of America's endless wars in the Middle East." Before 1990, American combat operations in the region had been generally temporary and short-term. Brookings Institute fellow Bruce Riedel explained in a 2024 article that "President George H. W. Bush wanted to continue that pattern when he responded forcefully and appropriately to Iraq's aggression, but it did not work out that way. Four presidents since have discovered it's hard to get out."

The new decade also brought some happier developments. David and Suzanne welcomed their son Michael to the world in 1990. Since Suzanne worked full-time and David was researching and writing from home, he was the primary caretaker. He was grateful for babysitting help from his brother Bob and parents Marge and Warren.

During this period David saw an advertisement for a one-year teaching position at St. Mary's College of Maryland, about one hundred miles from Columbia. The small liberal arts college was looking for an Asian specialist, which usually means a focus on China and East Asia. He looked at the college's course curriculum in the history department and noticed that Middle East history was not included. With Middle East tensions still a big international topic, he convinced the college to alter the job specifications and was hired as a full-time visiting professor. The year of teaching prepared him well for the rigorous academic endeavors that would come next, but the long hours in the classroom, coupled with the lengthy commute, were exhausting.

In 1991, doctorate in hand, David began to search for full-time tenure-track positions around the country. He found five universities advertising positions in Middle East history and applied to all of them: Skidmore College in New York, Kutztown University of Pennsylvania, the University of North Texas, Stetson University in Florida, and Trinity University in Texas. He was offered a faculty position by all of them, but his favorite—Trinity University—was a little slower in its decision. More than a hundred people had applied, and by December the candidate field had been narrowed to ten. As one of those finalists, David was invited to attend the American Historical Association conference in Chicago in January 1992, where several members of the Trinity search committee planned to conduct interviews with leading candidates. Three would be chosen for a campus visit and more interviews.

Trinity University is a private liberal arts college with more than 2,600 students and 300 faculty members, all with advanced degrees, located on a sprawling campus in San Antonio, the seventh-largest city in the United States. From rather humble beginnings, Trinity is ranked today among the country's top liberal arts colleges by *U.S. News & World Report*. Established in 1869 by the Presbyterian Church in Tehuacana, Texas, about eighty-five miles from Dallas and an hour's ride by horseback from the closest railroad station, the original campus consisted of a two-story house with eight rooms. When its doors opened that fall, there were seven students and five faculty members. It relocated to San Antonio in 1942, and by the 1980s and 1990s visionary changes were shaping the university into a highly competitive and nationally outstanding institution.

Ron Calgaard became the university's president in 1979. He was a prescient leader who focused on strategic fundraising, intense recruitment of a top-tier faculty and student body, and innovative curriculum development. By the time David Lesch submitted his application, Calgaard had attracted several nationally respected scholars to the faculty. One of those was British historian Colin Wells, who became the first T. Frank Murchison Distinguished Professor of Classical Studies in 1987. With multiple degrees from Oxford University, he specialized in ancient Roman history and published several groundbreaking books on that subject. Because he also was a prominent archaeologist, he participated in the excavations at Carthage from 1976 to 1986, which brought some star power to Trinity. Another standout figure, political scientist John Stoessinger, had studied with Henry Kissinger while completing his doctorate at Harvard, had been the acting director for the United Nations Political Affairs Division, and was the author of more than ten award-winning books, including *Henry Kissinger: The Anguish of Power*. David knew he would be joining an impressive cadre if Trinity hired him.

The university reserved a large suite in the hotel where the academic conference was being held. David arrived for his interview dressed in his customary jacket, tie, and charcoal gray pants. John McCusker, one of the faculty members charged with interviewing him, welcomed him warmly, putting the young applicant at ease. McCusker was a recent hire, the school's first Ewing Halsell Distinguished Professor of American History and a professor of economics. He had studied as an undergraduate with Nobel Laureate Robert Fogel at the University of Rochester, did graduate research at the University of London, earned his doctorate at the University of Pittsburgh, and taught for more than twenty years at the University of Maryland, College Park. He already had authored five books, epitomizing Ron Calgaard's drive to bring the best to Trinity.

"David carried himself well," McCusker recalls today, "and he had good answers to the questions we asked. But he was younger than the other applicants and some of Trinity's older professors were hesitant; perhaps they felt their territory was being threatened. But he came, he saw, and he conquered. David is not the type to ever shrink from a challenge. He was true to his motto, 'Never eliminate yourself,' and he was hired."

As David prepared to move to San Antonio, Texas, there was movement in the Middle East as well. More than one million Jews relocated to Israel from Russia and the Eastern bloc countries when restrictions were lifted in 1991. There were also several dramatic airlifts of Ethiopian Jews to Israel that year. As new citizens poured into that prosperous country, most others in the region were experiencing social and economic strains as results of the Gulf War. Even nations not involved in the fighting suffered as weather patterns were disrupted, black rain from oil residues destroyed crops, and decreased oil production wreaked havoc on economies. The situation was so dire that nations in the region began to consider ways they might work together to alleviate it. On October 30, 1991, Israeli, Syrian, Jordanian, Lebanese, and Palestinian delegations attended the Madrid Peace Conference, cosponsored by the United States and Russia. The result was a two-track process calling for separate bilateral talks involving the conference participants and intended to produce new peace treaties. There also would be multilateral negotiations aimed at "building the Middle East of the future." It was that story—the rich, complex history of a troubled region and possibilities in the years ahead—that David would bring to college students at Trinity. Together they would watch future events unfold in the Middle East.

Trinity University, San Antonio, Texas

In early August 1992 David came to San Antonio with two-year-old Michael while Suzanne stayed in Maryland to wind down her work commitments at the Social Security Administration. John McCusker and his wife, Ann Van Pelt, were especially welcoming, inviting the family to dinner in their home and creating a bond with David that would last a lifetime. David admired McCusker's academic experience and expertise and was grateful for his mentorship and friendship. And McCusker saw in David a young assistant professor who had some special character traits that would prove invaluable in the competitive world of academia.

Fittingly, David would become the Ewing Halsell Distinguished Professor of History at Trinity University when McCusker retired several decades later.

Success in that world is based on simple but demanding achievements. Within the first six years as a member of the faculty, publication of a book is highly recommended. The old saying "publish or perish" remains true. David published his first book in 1992, titled *Syria and the United States: Eisenhower's Cold War in the Middle East* and based on his dissertation, less than a year after he arrived at Trinity. Additional publications, a strong teaching record, and professional and community service earned him the promotion to associate professor and tenure in 1997.

Just as he had done while attending Harvard and teaching at St. Mary's College, David found ways to earn extra money during the summer. During his first year at Trinity he met an entrepreneurial real estate developer, Williston Clover, who spotted the professor's intelligence and writing skills right away. Clover had made money and friends all over the world—first as the co-owner of Panorama with his father in the 1970s, followed by his purchase of the Gramercy Park Hotel in New York; development projects in Cancún, Mexico, in its nascent days of tourism; and a myriad of consultancies in Belize, Costa Rica, Saint Lucia, Saudi Arabia, Houston, and finally San Antonio. He hired David to study and critique a project he called "Wild West San Antonio." His first attempt at analyzing it was not quite what Clover wanted, and the two sat down to discuss it. Many decades later, eighty-three-year-old Clover described how carefully David listened, how open he was to a different approach, and how brilliant his final submission was. The two men became lifelong friends, and in the years ahead Clover would introduce his protégé to important people in his new hometown and far beyond.

In the meantime David was on a fast track to being promoted

to full professor. Some of Trinity's older associate professors were wary of the thirty-something whiz kid who was already planning another book and an international conference about the Middle East that would bring attention to the university in extraordinary ways. When he began receiving acceptances from high-profile scholars and diplomats around the world, jealousies surfaced in some of his colleagues and caused friction within the history department. McCusker was also resented by some for being the department's first distinguished professor. The resentment both men felt on opposite ends of the academic hierarchy helped solidify their friendship. McCusker remembers those difficult times and praises David for never being defeated by the situation, saying, "He just moved on. That is his character." David likened the tension in the history department at Trinity to athletics, where players fail all the time but focus on the next thing—getting a next at bat, pitching the next out, trying to sink the next basket. "Hall of Famers in basketball are right 50 percent of the time. In baseball, 30 percent of the time," he told McCusker. "I can get through this."

As he planned the conference, good news seemed to be unfolding in the Middle East. With the signing of the Oslo I Accord in the fall of 1993, a new hope for peace made its tentative entrance on the world stage. In September Yasser Arafat, chairman of the PLO, and Yitzhak Rabin, prime minister of Israel, agreed to a Declaration of Principles (DOP) negotiated in Oslo, Norway. The agreement outlined an Israeli redeployment from parts of the occupied West Bank and Gaza Strip and the establishment of a provisional Palestinian self-rule government. Both sides agreed to recognize each other publicly. A month later President Bill Clinton hosted a ceremony for the two leaders in Washington, with an official signing of the Declaration of Principles that had emerged from the Oslo meetings. The following year Arafat

84 DODGERS TO DAMASCUS

and Rabin were awarded the Nobel Peace Prize along with Israel's president, Shimon Peres.

The Palestinian reaction was mixed. Some aligned themselves with the more extreme Islamist faction, and most Palestinian refugees in Lebanon, Syria, and Jordan rejected the agreement. The inhabitants of the territories most affected, however, seemed to welcome Arafat's promise of peace and economic well-being. These developments would spark important discussions at David Lesch's upcoming conference. There was even the wildly optimistic possibility that true peace for the Middle East might be on the horizon.

A title for the conference was chosen—"The Middle East and the United States: An Historical Inquiry"—and David secured the participation of a knighted British diplomat, Sir Samuel Falle. As Sir Roger Carrick explains in the foreword to Falle's autobiography, *My Lucky Life: In War, Revolution, Peace, and Diplomacy*, "Sam Falle earned himself a remarkable reputation inside the Diplomatic Service—as a political analyst, fearless and frank adviser, linguist, egalitarian, excellent man in a crisis, unstuffy Head of Mission, and an amusing, physically and morally tough colleague of great integrity." Who better to top the list of speakers in San Antonio in 1994?

Falle's life story reads like the best adventure novel. During World War II in 1942, while he was serving in the Royal Navy, his ship was sunk by the Japanese fleet during the Battle of the Java Sea. As a prisoner-of-war he endured three years of unimaginable torture at the hands of the camp's Kempeitai (military police) sergeant and was later awarded the Distinguished Service Cross for his bravery in battle and his leadership in the POW camp. Like a real-life James Bond, he joined His Majesty's Foreign Service (now the Diplomatic Service). His postings in the Middle East were dangerous and dramatic, including an expulsion from

Iran and a narrow escape from Iraq as revolution exploded there. He went on to serve as the UK's ambassador to Kuwait and Sweden and as high commissioner in Singapore and Nigeria. He was first knighted Knight Commander of the Royal Victorian Order by Queen Elizabeth in 1972 and Knight Commander of the Most Distinguished Order of Saint Michael and Saint George in the New Year Honours of 1979.

David met Falle in Austin while attending a Middle East conference at the University of Texas and recognized Falle's star power immediately. As he planned his first international conference two years later, he knew Falle's presence would be a highlight. He did not hesitate to reach out, relying on the "Never eliminate yourself" motto that had gotten him this far. Falle accepted the invitation to be a keynote speaker, and a lifelong friendship that would include many adventures in the UK and the Middle East began. Another keynote speaker was Yair Hirschfeld, an Israeli scholar who secretly orchestrated the peace talks between Israel and the PLO in Norway that led directly to the Oslo I Accord in 1993. Other important historians, authors, political scientists, and former diplomats joined the growing list of illustrious speakers, including Robert Freedman, who had awarded David that rare A-plus grade as an undergraduate and encouraged him to apply for a doctorate at Harvard.

David invited many of his Harvard buddies and newer academic friends, including Robert Satloff, Paul Kingston, James Gelvin, F. Gregory Gause III, Joshua Landis, Malik Mufti, Shafeeq Ghabra, Erika Alin, Sussan Siavoshi, and Fawaz Gerges. Many were relatively unknown at the time but soon became successful scholars, authors, and policymakers. For most, the conference offered their first grand stage and significant publication, since each of them contributed a chapter to David's 1996 book, *The Middle East and the United States: A Historical and Political Reassessment*.

Trinity University president Ron Calgaard and David Lesch, 1994

Eventually more than forty presenters exchanged ideas during the three-day event, which was open to Trinity students and the public. Well-known former diplomats and scholars, including William Quandt, Gary Sick, Ambassador Alfred Leroy (Roy) Atherton, Ambassador Richard Bordeaux Parker, John Duke Anthony, Yvonne Haddad, Mohamed Sid-Ahmed, Georgiy Mirsky (foreign policy adviser to Mikhail Gorbachev), and Amatzia Baram, traveled to San Antonio that spring to share wide-ranging opinions about the most conflicted regions in the world.

Longtime Trinity University trustee Flora Cameron Crichton, whose passion in life was world affairs, funded the conference. It was a home run for Trinity University, and the first event of its kind on the campus. Student enrollment now surpassed two thousand, and its faculty possessed some of the country's best academic credentials. Innovative teaching styles and increasing diversity added to its strong educational heartbeat. San Antonio was now home base for David, Suzanne, and son Michael. Recognizing that he was well on his way toward tenure, David prepared for the challenges ahead. Wins and losses were to come in the rigors of academic life and in the tumultuous world of the Middle East, and David had found his home base in San Antonio, Texas.

HORIZONS OF HISTORY

As David crossed the tree-lined walkway toward the red brick building of the history department, he smiled at students scurrying to find their first class, noting that some looked flustered, even lost, on Trinity's spacious campus. The Calvert Bells in Murchison Tower rang out—heard as either melodious or ominous, depending on whether a given student had time to grab a coffee or was running late for an 8 a.m. class. Later that day David would meet more than fifty mostly first years and sophomores and half that number of upper division students who were focusing on the modern history of Syria, the modern history of the Persian Gulf, US diplomatic history, or US foreign policy in the Middle East. He chuckled as he remembered Abraham Lincoln's famous words, "We cannot escape history." His students were about to discover that truth, and he relished the discussions ahead.

The lower-division course began with a short survey. Students were asked to list a few words that described the Middle East and to fill in its countries on a blank map. The exercise took longer than David expected, and just two words dominated the answers: "oil" and "terrorism." He realized that the map exercise would have to wait until later in the semester, once his course had revealed more about what was an unknown part of the world for most college-age Americans in 1995.

Closer to home, in downtown San Antonio, the legendary River Walk offered students a chance to explore the new worlds that college life presents. Along the festive waterway, strolling mariachi musicians serenaded them and colorful bars provided the chance to test their borrowed IDs. Five historic Spanish missions built along the river in the eighteenth century reflected the city's unique multicultural history. The limestone walls and acequias that functioned as early waterways in the 1700s and 1800s were the oldest construction they had ever seen. David knew that learning about the ancient history of the Middle East would add a new perspective to their definition of old. And he was sure that his course on the Middle East's complex modern history would convince them how important the region would be in their twentieth-century world and in the years to come.

Ansel Stein ended up in the class by chance. As one of the last students to register for the fall semester, he chose Medieval Islamic History because it was one of the few courses that began at a decent hour and still had a few seats left. He remembered his professor nonchalantly mentioning on the first day that he had memorized all the caliphs in the Umayyad and Abbasid empires. Stein feared the road ahead would be challenging. But when the professor continued with a chuckle, Stein sighed with relief, realizing there was a touch of humor in the tall, well-dressed figure behind the lectern. When David began to outline the reasons the Middle East was so important, Stein was hooked, as much by David's passionate teaching style as by the information.

"You were right about the importance of oil in the Middle East," David told the first-year students. "With two-thirds of the world's reserves in the region, can you imagine what that means in our combustion-age world?" A few students raised their hands and were complimented for daring to participate in that first day's dialogue. David went on to ask them why all three of the great religions of the world—Judaism, Christianity, and Islam—originated in the Middle East. Not many hands went up, but they would find out soon enough. He showed them the blank map again, illustrating the region's geostrategic location linking Europe and Asia and Africa, a true crossroads of civilization. He juxtaposed stories about nomadic traders traveling by camel in ancient times with news articles about modern entrepreneurs in Dubai, now the world's largest free trade zone, visible today from space. The people and cultures of the Middle East began to come to life, and Stein and the other students began a journey of discovery, one that for some would result in careers in government, international business, cybersecurity, and even the CIA.

The course on Syria began its journey with a photographic overview that immersed students in the vast landscape of the desert and the ancient structures that had seen dramas unfold for millennia. The magnificent Roman ruins at Palmyra, the breathtaking Umayyad Mosque in Damascus, the Krak des Chevaliers crusader castle, the Mamluk Citadel of Aleppo, the norias (waterwheels) in Hama, and Ottoman-era structures—mosques, caravanserais, mausoleums, and palaces designed by Suleiman the Magnificent's renowned architect, Mimar Sinan—created a new definition of "old." They illustrated a rich and nuanced past shaped by diverse cultures and powerful rulers, culminating with the Ottoman Empire's stronghold on the country, which ended as a result of World War I.

David told his students that postwar negotiations regarding the Middle East were crafty and complex. The Entente Powers, including Britain, France, Italy, the United States, and other countries—proposed a wide variety of plans for determining the region's fate. He shared those nation-building challenges with

Temple of Baal, Palmyra, Syria

his students, along with historic photographs of Winston Churchill and Lawrence of Arabia (T. E. Lawrence) meeting in Cairo with Jordan's Emir Abdullah I and maps of the region before it was comprised of the countries we know today. The historic upheavals and political engineering that changed the Middle East would be documented in many of his future books, including *The Arab-Israeli Conflict: A History* in 2007 and *A History of the Middle East Since the Rise of Islam* in 2022.

Of course, part of the story David outlined involved oil, just as his students had guessed when asked to describe the Middle East on their first day of class. When the Entente Powers apportioned the Arab world between Britain and France, vast oil reserves were the prize. Britain took Palestine (including present-day Jordan) and Mesopotamia, and its status in Egypt and the Persian Gulf continued. France was assigned the Syrian mandate, including

Lebanon. The former provinces of the once huge Ottoman Empire, where Bedouins, Edomites, Semites, and other Arab tribes had inhabited the desert for millennia, were delineated into new states. Despite the diversity of the sects involved, nearly all were hostile to the new arbitrary borders and the division they caused. In Syria there were uprisings and unrest for the next two decades as it tried to shape its modern persona. What happened there after World War II was precisely David's field of expertise, informing the subject of his doctoral dissertation at Harvard and his first published book, and creating the basis for one of the most popular history courses at Trinity University.

Immediately following the war, France tried to retain its control over Syria, ironically bombing Damascus while Syrian prime minister Fares al-Khoury was in San Francisco participating in the conference that resulted in the formation of the United Nations. But in 1946 Syria gained its independence and officially became a nation-state. David could not wait to share that story with his students and to dive deep into Syria's modern history. He designed his courses to fuel curiosity and expand his students' worldview, remembering the inspiration and mentorship professors like Freedman, Cantori, Safran, Khoury, and others had given him. He took care to build in time for class discussion and opportunities for discourse outside the classroom, and he learned to add a bit of showmanship to capture his students' attention.

Former student Ulrico "Rico" Izaguirre recognized the special energy that permeated David's courses and found himself pondering ways he might harness it to design his future beyond the university. "Given the world climate at the time—with the newly signed Oslo Accords adding hope to the Middle East peace process—you could not help but feel you were close to a guy who was trying to make something historic and world-changing happen," he says. "To have someone with such deep knowledge and engagement on this subject made going to class with him something extraordinary."

Still enjoying the afterglow of the successful international conference he organized during his first year at Trinity, David began to think of ways to establish the university as an important center for Middle East studies. He knew that the conference's sponsor, Flora Cameron Crichton, was a close friend of George H. W. Bush, as was David Bates, an aide to the former president whom he often saw in San Antonio. With their encouragement and assistance, David approached the former president about creating an institute that would bear his name and facilitate academic, business, cultural, and political cooperation between the United States and the nations and people of the Middle East. In one of Bush's first of many letters to David, he addressed him by his first name and wrote, "Please excuse the informality, but anybody who was the number one draft pick for the Dodgers is probably used to such treatment." The former president agreed to lend his name to the proposed project, but he warned David that he was focusing his time and all fundraising efforts on his presidential library, under construction at Texas A&M University.

The two men exchanged wonderful letters discussing events happening in the baseball world and events going on in the Middle East. In early 1996 David helped arrange a meeting between Bush and Syria's president Hafez al-Assad in Damascus. David received confidential correspondence suggesting that Assad was interested in the possibility of meeting Bush during the former president's planned trip to Bahrain and the United Arab Emirates to commemorate the fifth anniversary of the Gulf War. Mohammad Ali Hourieh, president of the University of Aleppo and a childhood friend of Assad, and Elias Samo, director of the school's international relations department, both of whom

David had befriended during his summer in Syria in 1995, began the secret exploratory inquiry. David was delighted when Bush added Syria to his March travel schedule.

"I only wish you had more time to spend in Syria," David wrote to Bush, "because it is truly one of those crossroads of history whose archaeological and historical sites are second to none in the Middle East, or in the entire world for that matter. But the meeting between yourself and Assad is a wonderful occasion that can only improve US-Syrian relations and the chances of a comprehensive peace in the region, the prospects for which you were responsible for making." The two world leaders had a positive meeting, and both remained committed to the ongoing Madrid peace process.

David continued to work on the establishment of the George Bush Institute for Middle East Studies at Trinity and created a prospectus describing its goals and the reasons for naming it for Bush. It praised the former president as "a world leader who was primarily responsible for creating a more positive environment in the Middle East and in the Arab-Israeli and Persian Gulf arenas as a result of both actions taken during the Gulf crisis and war of 1990–1991 and the initiatives that have worked toward a comprehensive Arab-Israeli peace." David traveled to Washington to meet Arab ambassadors and to the Persian Gulf to speak with high-level officials in an effort to raise the necessary funding. But the timing was not right, and fundraising efforts were thwarted by the massive campaign underway for the George H. W. Bush Presidential Library and Museum in College Station, Texas, which opened in 1997, with a construction cost of $43 million. Donations were received from supporters throughout the United States, Europe, and the Middle East. Today the library, museum, and conference center attract more than 250,000 visitors each year. Although the institute at Trinity was never established,

Bush remained a staunch supporter of both David's work and Trinity's achievements in the academic world, especially as he was an emeritus trustee at the school.

In 1999 Bush presented the annual Flora Cameron Lecture in Politics and Public Affairs to a packed house in Trinity's 2,700-seat Laurie Auditorium. David arranged for him to speak earlier in the day to his US diplomatic history class, and the forty students there enjoyed the thrill of meeting the former president and hearing his insights. Israel's prime minister Shimon Peres also came to campus that same year. Rico Izaguirre, who was about to graduate, said he and his classmates could see that "David was part of the leadership trying to make a lasting peace for the betterment of mankind."

According to Izaguirre, the fact that David's knowledge extended beyond academics gave his classes a legitimacy and a hands-on perspective that his students recognized as unique. When David offered Izaguirre the opportunity to participate in the Model Arab League, sponsored by the National Council on US-Arab Relations, he accepted with enthusiasm, serving first as a delegate and then as the assistant secretary general for the statewide youth leadership program. Inspired by the experience, he and several other students organized an international fraternity on Trinity's campus, with members hailing from Mexico, Palestine, Iran, Iraq, and Bahrain. David served as its sponsor. "Having close friends who were personally impacted by events in the Middle East was especially important for me," Izaguirre says, "and frankly we liked the fact that we were more worldly than the typical American—and very homogenous—Greek fraternity offerings at the time."

After graduating from Trinity in 1999 with a bachelor's degree in political science and a double minor in history and international studies, Izaguirre headed for the White House, where he was an aide for Vice President Al Gore and later worked on his presidential campaign. Over the next few years he worked on other political campaigns, including Kathleen Kennedy Townsend's run for governor of Maryland and Jan Laverty Jones's run for governor of Nevada. When Jones lost her election, she was hired by Caesars Entertainment, the country's largest gaming company, and Izaguirre joined her there, specializing in the complex national and international licensing end of the most regulated business in the country. Today he is chief public affairs officer at Manifest Financial, a company that offers tailored financial solutions for entrepreneurs and the platforms they use, boosting their engagement in the creator economy.

Joe Balat was a close friend during Izaguirre's university days and a cofounder of the international fraternity. As a first-generation Palestinian American, he enrolled in David's course as a freshman in 1997, when fellow Palestinian student Christian Elhaj advised him there was a professor at Trinity whose sole objective was educating college students about the Middle East. He remembers that during his college years—"the post-Oslo and pre-9/11 world"—the vitriol and stigma associated with the Middle East and its people had not yet escalated and that David's courses were challenging, interactive, and always taught without bias. His teaching style included a great deal of firsthand experience. Balat recognized how much that helped him gain perspective, and that perspective is "the first step to understanding conflict to take steps toward a potential resolution."

As David had done long ago in Robert Freedman's history class at the University of Maryland, his students often arrived early for his medieval Islamic history course to ask questions. Ansel Stein quickly changed his mind about the class he had been reluctant to take and credits it with changing his life path. He enthusiastically enrolled in David's modern Middle East

British prime minister John Major, center, with Trinity students and professors John McCusker and David Lesch, 1999

history course the next year. When he heard about the Summer in Syria program sponsored by the National Council on US-Arab Relations, he asked David about participating. Scholar and diplomat John Duke Anthony founded the organization in 1983 to work with students and the public to increase understanding of the Arab world. He wanted to focus on that region because it is the one the United States has mobilized and deployed more armed forces to than any other place since the 1980s. David led a group of students to Syria in 1995, and he and Anthony had become friends. Stein applied for the program, and David championed the application. Stein's experience in Syria was transformative. "No one in my family had ever been abroad before, and of course, no one could understand why I wanted to go to a region that was considered dangerous and exotic," Stein explains. "But I saw in Dr. Lesch someone I wanted to be like, and he encouraged me to take a risk. It was one of the most important events in my life."

David (fourth from right) with students in the Summer in Syria program sponsored by the National Council on U.S.-Arab Relations

During one of the summer sessions in 1995, David met a young man who was giving a lecture on developing technology in Syria. He was Bashar al-Assad, then president of the Syrian Computer Society, who had recently returned to Syria from London. He never dreamed that their paths would cross again within a decade, in ways that would change both men's lives. David's group of students traveled throughout the country, enjoying access to many sites requiring government approval, including the sacred Sayyida Zaynab Mosque in Damascus. Zaynab bint Ali and her brother Husayn ibn Ali were the grandchildren of the Prophet Muhammad. Husayn was killed at the Battle of Karbala in 680 CE by the Umayyad Caliphate army; Zaynab died shortly after in 682. Husayn's martyrdom is considered the "big bang" of Shiite Islam that galvanized the growth of that now powerful religious sect. In 1995 only Shiite Muslims were allowed to visit the shrine, but David's group obtained special permission. The students also visited the Golan Heights and waved to Israeli soldiers on the other side, and they marveled at the Noria al-Muhammadiyya, a giant waterwheel built in Hama in 1361 CE.

After graduating in 2000 with a double major in history and religion/anthropology, Ansel Stein earned a master's degree in international relations and religion from Boston University. He joined the CIA as an analyst, intent on pursuing his professor's dream of helping the government understand and better relate to the Middle East. "I got from Dr. Lesch a sense of earnest appreciation for the people of the region and the realization that understanding people and their governments was essential. I did my best to emulate that," Stein says. He went on to serve in the US State Department as an economic officer focusing on the Middle East, served in the US embassy in Abu Dhabi, founded Thorntree Intelligence, and serves as the chief analyst for Crisis24, a global company that specializes in security and risk-management services.

During the more than twenty years since their graduations, Stein, Balat, and Izaguirre have worked with David on electoral, business, and development projects, some involving Syria. They consider their former professor a close friend and mentor, the ultimate praise for someone who believes in the powerful and lasting impact of education. But they also remember that not everyone did well in David's classes. Students who did not do their reading or came to class unprepared probably longed for an escape. But by the end of each semester a major shift would occur. Despite the complexity of the course's subject matter, students were collectively captivated and their evaluations described David as "brilliant," "demanding but exceptionally fair," and "a great listener." Stein remembers that David's "oblique references about going to Washington for meetings at the White House" added a wonderful touch of intrigue and inspired students to pay attention. Syria became a real place and now easy to locate on a map of the Middle East.

They studied the effects of its old strategic alliances and explored the impacts of its dramatic shifts in leadership. When they analyzed the pact that Syria made with the Soviet Union in 1956—in exchange for planes, tanks, and military equipment—the modern relationship between the two countries became understandable. They also explored the country's political unrest during the 1960s and the momentous change that occurred in 1970 when an army general named Hafez al-Assad carried out a bloodless military coup. He assumed the role of president, an office he would hold for the next thirty years, and his larger-than-life persona made him a fascinating character study in class. In Arabic al-Assad means "the lion," but the president's family had not always possessed this rather glorious name. Originally it was al-Wahhish—which in Arabic means "the beast"—until Hafez's father, Ali ibn Sulayman, changed it in 1927, three years before Hafez was born. The class read Assad's biography, written by David's colleague Patrick Seale, and observed that the older surname still seemed to fit a leader who was known for his brutality.

The Assads were Alawites, an offshoot of Shiite Islam that is considered by most Muslims to be heretical. The thirteenth-century scholar Ibn Taymiyya issued a fatwa—a legal ruling—calling the Alawites greater infidels than Christians, Jews, or idolaters. In a country that is 75 percent Sunni Muslim, Alawites have long been a minority, along with the Christians and the Druze. But large numbers volunteered and were recruited into the Syrian armed forces during French governance in the 1920s, and eventually those Alawite officers gained political influence. Hafez was one of those individuals, enlisting in the military air academy, graduating as a pilot, and eventually achieving

Syrian president Hafez al-Assad with his family, circa 1970

positions as commander of the air force and minister of defense in the mid-1960s. His wife, Anisa Makhlouf, was his first cousin and part of one of the most powerful Alawite families in Syria. Some say her relatives came to control 60 percent of the country's economy, with major holdings in the country's banking, oil, and telecommunications sectors, ensuring that the al-Assads always were well-financed. They had five children, all born in the 1960s and still quite young when their forty-year-old father assumed the presidency in 1970. Three years later the family moved from a modest condominium-like home in the historic center of Damascus to a new home in the upscale Malki district, where a number of embassies and consulates are located today.

A new constitution in 1973 led to a national crisis when the Assad regime removed the requirement that Syria's president be a Muslim, hoping to put to rest any doubts about an Alawite president. Fierce demonstrations in Homs, Hama, and Aleppo erupted and protestors there labeled Assad "the enemy of Allah."

Author and international relations expert Robert D. Kaplan has compared Hafez al-Assad's improbable rise to "an untouchable becoming maharajah in India or a Jew becoming tsar in Russia."

Opponents of the Assad government were inspired by the Iranian revolution, where an Islamist movement successfully overthrew what it considered to be a non-Islamic regime, and the assassination of Anwar Sadat by Islamic Group recruits made Assad even more aware of his vulnerability. He responded like a lion, or perhaps a beast. As fundamentalist opposition from the Muslim Brotherhood continued, with much of it centered in Hama, the Assad government leveled parts of that city in 1982, killing between ten thousand and thirty thousand people. During the rest of Assad's thirty-year reign, public demonstrations against the government were rare. When his younger brother Rifaat al-Assad attempted a coup in 1984, he was promptly expelled from Syria, lived in exile in France for the next thirty-six years, and was eventually found guilty of stealing millions of euros from the Syrian state. The country's economy was in shambles, corruption was rampant, and internal conflicts simmered. David's classes at Trinity studied and discussed how and why those unfolding dramas led Syria to make the surprising strategic choice to join the Arab-Israeli peace process, something it had avoided for decades. Another surprise was on Syria's horizon as well.

It had long been accepted that Bassel al-Assad, the eldest son of Syria's president, would inherit the leadership of the country. But one foggy morning in 1994 he was killed in a car accident just outside the Damascus airport. That cold January day Bashar al-Assad, the second eldest son, was in his London apartment when he received the news that his older brother had died. A licensed ophthalmologist who had graduated from Damascus University, Bashar was studying for a postgraduate degree at the Western Eye Hospital. He promptly returned to Syria to support his grieving family and to assist with the funeral arrangements, never imaging what his future held.

During David's first few years teaching at Trinity, major events in the Middle East shook the region and beyond. Israeli prime minister Yitzhak Rabin was assassinated by a right-wing opponent of the peace process in 1995. The following year Israel freed thousands of Palestinian prisoners. Iraq agreed to enter talks about a new United Nations plan to allow the sale of $1 billion of Iraqi oil, with proceeds earmarked for humanitarian purposes. More than a hundred civilians were killed in Lebanon when Israel Defense Forces bombs accidentally hit the United Nations compound. In other parts of the world dramas were exploding on every continent, from the end of apartheid in South Africa to the trial of Cambodia's notorious leader Pol Pot.

Closer to home, things were calmer. David and Suzanne built a new house in a fast-growing suburb of north-central San Antonio and joined The Club at Sonterra so their son Michael could learn to swim, a necessity for enduring the hot Texas summers. David picked up an old tennis racket he had kept since his college days and headed for the club's state-of-the-art courts. Decades earlier he had played with his older brother, Bob, who always beat him, before baseball and basketball dominated his sports life. Once he was drafted by the Dodgers, he was instructed to stop playing tennis as it put too much pressure on his pitching arm. When he returned to the courts nearly twenty years later, the club's tennis pro, Richard Walthall, laughed when he saw David's outdated wooden racket, noting he had not seen one like it in fifteen years. Soon David had a new fiberglass racket in hand, and he rediscovered a game he had once loved. His booming serve, a remnant of his once famous ninety-mile-per-hour fastball, quickly took him to the club pro level, and tennis became a happy outlet for both his competitive spirit and gregarious personality.

Michael Lesch,
Christmas 1997

Michael was happy attending the all-new schools in what was one of the city's most modern neighborhoods: first Stone Oak Elementary School, then Barbara Bush Middle School, and Ronald Reagan High School. With a cohort of good friends, he played baseball, basketball and, of course, the popular role-playing game Dungeons & Dragons. David jumped right into action, shooting hoops and playing catch with the boys, coaching their sports teams, and competing on the Nintendo Game Boy. Michael was master of the video-game universe. His father David never could beat him and marveled at the innovation that birthed the technology revolution. Summer trips to Maryland were idyllic and provided a chance for Michael to see his grandparents, uncle Bob and his wife Laurie, and cousins, and for David and Suzanne to reconnect with old friends.

As the only grandchild on the Lesch side of the family, Michael was the center of attention whenever he visited Maryland. Warren and Margaret doted on him, and the dense woods behind their home presented him with a peaceful kingdom to explore. The magic was multiplied during Christmas vacations in Bel Air. Warren and Margaret recreated the routine David had known as a boy: a festive Christmas Eve dinner with the entire family, holiday carols playing on the stereo, a lavishly decorated tree with sparkling lights and too many presents to count, and ultimately Michael's excited approach to the living room the next morning, where he discovered a huge array of surprises from Santa Claus. In 1997 seven-year-old Michael was fully outfitted with new baseball gear; the year's hottest toy—a handheld digital pet named Tamagotchi—was in his stocking; a bright red bicycle was waiting outside. Warren tossed baseballs, pretended to like the computerized egg-shaped toy, held his grandson's bike as he pushed off to new adventures, and relived moments he had shared with David when he was a boy. Just two months later Warren died of a heart attack. That Christmas holiday was etched in David's heart forever, and the memory of his father's joy on that cold morning in Maryland was a powerful source of comfort during the grieving process in 1998 and beyond.

David's professional life in the late 1990s included international business consultancies. Several Fortune 500 companies, including Enron, Stewart & Stevenson, and Motorola, recognized David's vast connections in the Middle East and enlisted his talents as they pursued diverse ideas for businesses. David and former president Bush continued to correspond on Middle East initiatives and their shared love of baseball. As George W. Bush prepared to follow in his father's political footsteps, David offered to help. Students in his Trinity classes enjoyed their inside-track exposure to fascinating letters and diplomatic endeavors that took their history courses to a whole new level. As the new millennium approached, a remarkable surge of interest and trepidation in the historic moment began to build.

Worldwide media coverage added to the excitement and angst, which included anticipated computer errors during the calendar year change—popularly called the Y2K problem. Businesses and government organizations created technology teams to ensure that all hardware and software were prepared. Some people stocked up on food, water, and firearms, purchased backup generators, and withdrew large sums from their banks.

In the summer of 1999 David taught a course on US foreign policy toward the Middle East, and one suggested term paper topic was "the greatest threats to the United States." The class could choose from a list of possibilities. Joe Balat and two friends selected Osama bin Laden and the growing threat of the militant Islamist group al-Qaeda. David recalls that he awarded their chilling presentation a high grade, and two years later their assessment of that major threat proved true. Balat has never forgotten that course.

Events in 1999, including the death of King Hussein of Jordan, an earthquake in Turkey that killed more than seventeen thousand people, and big troubles in Syria were perceived by citizens in those countries as precursors of Y2K's predicted disasters. Late that year violent protests and armed clashes left hundreds dead or injured in the Syrian village of Latakia, where David had shared drinks in 1989 with Russian navy officers the night before their ship exploded. Reports of President Hafez al-Assad's increasingly fragile health added to unease in the troubled region. David's students at Trinity were more concerned with ominous international events like these than by the futuristic doomsday scenarios of Y2K. And they were right. January 1, 2000, arrived without incident. The internet did not crash, and planes did not fall out of the sky.

In May, despite his declining health, Assad traveled to Geneva for meetings with President Bill Clinton, who hoped to persuade the Syrian leader to restart peace talks with Israel and prevent renewed violence in the Middle East. *The Guardian* reported that the talks started warmly enough, with the two leaders smiling and shaking hands. But Israeli prime minister Ehud Barak told a cabinet meeting in Jerusalem that he rated Clinton's chances of salvaging the peace process as no higher than 50 percent. Syria's state-controlled newspaper, *Al-Thawra*, cautioned that "most of the political forces in Israel are not mature enough for a just peace." Some international observers believed Assad was making the effort to save his son, Bashar—then his expected successor—from inheriting the ongoing conflict. Others held the view that his efforts were half-hearted and that he was glad to leave the problem of peace to Bashar. Most agreed that Clinton was hoping to enhance his presidential legacy as the end of his final term in office approached. Whatever the two leaders' intentions were, the summit overlooking peaceful Lake Geneva failed to produce an agreement. Just a little over a month later Hafez al-Assad died, plunging the region into deep and potentially dangerous uncertainty.

David would describe these times in the many books he wrote over the next decades. In his 2012 book *Syria: The Fall of the House of Assad*, he explained that "Assad became somewhat of a puppeteer, manipulating the diverse set of groups in the country and often playing them against one another; indeed by the time he died in 2000, there were some 17 different intelligence agencies in Syria with overlapping portfolios that the grand master would utilize to be sure no one pocket of state authority became too independent or powerful."

On June 11, 2000, one day after the death of the "puppeteer," the ruling Ba'ath Party nominated Bashar as president. There were no other nominees. The national assembly hastily amended the Syrian constitution, changing the minimum age required to be president from forty to thirty-four years old—the exact age of Bashar, who was born on September 11, 1965. In a nationwide referendum he received 97.29 percent of the total vote. He was elected and delivered his inaugural speech in Damascus on July 17. In a subtle fashion, he seemed to lay the foundation for embarking on a different path from his father, suggesting that "we must rid ourselves of those old ideas that have become obstacles. In order to succeed we need modern thinking." David's students analyzed the speech, discussing what the new president's vision might mean for Syria.

There was a genuine exuberance among international policymakers who had longed to see change in Syria. Some even dared to attach the word "reformer" to Bashar al-Assad. David saw the importance of the moment and began to envision a remarkable opportunity. Perhaps he could approach this young leader about writing his biography, just as Patrick Seale had done for Bashar's father. The result might be a story that would engage Western readers, giving them a new understanding of Syria and the Middle East in general. But before David's idea could move forward, a terrorist attack on the United States on September 11, 2001, brought the Middle East into focus in a terrible way.

Along with most Americans and others around the world, David's students were profoundly shocked when two airplanes hijacked by al-Qaeda terrorists flew into the Twin Towers of the World Trade Center in New York. A third plane hit the Pentagon just outside Washington, and a fourth crashed in an empty field in Pennsylvania, presumably headed for the White House or the US Capitol. More than three thousand people were killed in the deadliest terror attacks in American history, and in the years that followed thousands of first responders and others working near the site where the Twin Towers once stood struggled with cancer and other chronic health problems from the toxicity of "Ground Zero."

The World Trade Center after being struck by two hijacked airliners, New York City, September 11, 2001

The morning of the attacks began as a lovely fall day in New England. Crisp temperatures and bright sun greeted people starting their workday. The staggered timing of the attacks ensured that millions watching the morning news on television would witness the horror as it unfolded. Video crews captured footage that both terrified and enraged the country and many parts of the larger international community. President George W. Bush was in Florida visiting an elementary school classroom when his chief of staff, Andrew Card, whispered the chilling news to the president. Bush later wrote about his response: "I made the decision not to jump up immediately and leave the classroom. I didn't want to rattle the kids. I wanted to project a sense of calm...I had been through enough crises to know that the first thing a leader has to do is project calm."

That evening Bush addressed the nation, still projecting calm but vowing retaliation against those responsible for carrying out

HORIZONS OF HISTORY

the attack. The US Congress quickly authorized military force, and the "war on terror" began with strikes in Afghanistan, believed to be the headquarters for al-Qaeda and its leader Osama bin Laden, and soon expanded to Iraq. Like most scholars of the Middle East, David realized that a new chapter had begun in the complex story of that troubled land.

He had just dropped Michael at school and stopped at home before heading to Trinity. As he gathered his papers, he turned on the television and saw the second tower of the World Trade Center explode. Michael and his classmates saw it too. Schools already in session tuned into television reports, and students witnessed people jumping from high floors to escape the fires. Classes at Trinity were canceled for the rest of the day. Several days later David and other colleagues who taught Middle East studies were asked to speak to the students in the university's 2,700-seat Laurie Auditorium. Every seat was filled. The professors wondered how to make sense of it all, how to explain that this was the work of a small group of extremist Muslims and not reflective of the religion of Islam and why some Arabs and Muslims were seen celebrating after the attack. At first David was frustrated and very angry. He knew there had been terrorist attacks by radical Islamists and Arabs prior to 9/11, including the Munich Olympics bombing in 1972, more than a dozen bombings in Paris in 1985, and the bombing of two US embassies in Tanzania and Kenya in 1998.

Until 9/11 he had spent his professional life defending Muslims and the Arab world from gross mischaracterizations, ignorance, and prejudice that were sparked by these events. The attacks in 2001 profoundly shook him. "As an American, and someone who considers himself a patriot, I was mad," he remembers. But later, as he watched vindictive caricatures of Arabs and Muslims emerge, accompanied by violence against them or anyone who

Umayyad Mosque, Damascus, Syria

looked like them, he called on his deeper intellectual roots to overcome the anger and focus on what he knew about the cultures he understood so well. But he admits it was a difficult test of his commitment at the time.

While the events of 9/11 and its aftermath dominated the American view of the Middle East in 2001, David did not lose sight of events unfolding in Syria under the administration of Bashar al-Assad. He even noted the eerie coincidence that Bashar's birthday was September 11. The president was part of the younger, modernizing generation in the Arab world, someone who had lived abroad and had an avowed affinity for Western pop music. Expectations in the West surrounding Bashar were optimistic. Recognizing a potentially positive—and possibly historic—new horizon for the Middle East, David revisited his earlier idea. It was bold, the time was right, and he was ready to write.

As usual, he created his plan with care, utilizing his deep knowledge of Syria and its history. In 2002 he wrote to Syria's minister of higher education, Ghias Barakat, who had become a good friend over the years. His letter was carefully crafted, recognizing Bashar's unusual rise to president and the promise that surrounded his future. He did not hear a word for two years, although he continued to travel to Syria and other countries in the Middle East for academic conferences and international consulting for projects ranging from a proposed power plant in Syria to an eighteen-hole golf resort in Oman. Then, in early 2004, the Syrian ambassador to the United States, Imad Moustapha, telephoned David in his office at Trinity. He simply said, "It's on." A trip to Syria was arranged for May, and David would soon find himself on the road to Damascus.

David Lesch with Syrian president Bashar al-Assad, 2004

IN THE LION'S DEN

On a warm day in May, in 2004, at exactly 7:30 a.m., the door opened to Bashar al-Assad's office in the Rowda Building in northwest Damascus. The president was standing just inside and greeted David warmly, extending his hand and welcoming him to Syria. Dressed in a dark blue suit and blue tie, the thirty-eight-year-old leader was tall—the same height as David—with piercing blue eyes and a gentle smile. He offered his guest a glass of freshly squeezed lemonade, and although his English was good, he introduced his translator, Nayef al-Yasin, a professor of English literature at Damascus University, who would make sure any of the president's Arabic words were correctly noted. David was not quite sure what to make of the man who opened his own door with a friendly smile.

Bashar's father had been notorious for keeping visitors waiting, sometimes for two or three hours, but David's first meeting with the president began exactly on time, an indication of a new leadership style. It had been expertly choreographed from the moment he arrived in Syria. A protocol officer from the president's office met his plane and ushered him into a VIP room, where he was served strong Arabic coffee while she took care of paperwork and his luggage. She accompanied him in the official sedan that sped through traffic to the Sheraton Hotel and advised him that the president's security detail would pick him up the next morning at seven o'clock. The president liked an early start to the day.

David was in the hotel's ornate waiting room when the protocol officers arrived, and he was escorted to one of the two official black sedans parked outside. Again, traffic pulled over for the presidential cars as they passed Umayyad Square, the Ministry of Defense, and the Al-Assad National Library, with its tall statue of Bashar's father guarding its gate. They stopped in front of a rather unremarkable building where two security officers, armed and dressed in black, stood by the entrance. Certain he would be searched, David prepared to show them the contents of his briefcase—a selection of his books, notepad and pens, and a small Sony tape recorder and portable microphone. To his surprise there was no examination of the briefcase, no metal detector to walk through, really no security at all.

The next surprise was Assad's presence at his own office door and his easy hospitality. The two men chatted briefly, and each recognized that the other had done his research prior to the meeting. Assad knew about David's baseball career and the books he had written about Syria, even joking that *Syria and the United States*, published in 1992, had been somewhat critical of his father. After a slightly awkward pause, the president suggested they start the interview, and David took out his tape recorder. "That won't be necessary," Assad said. Respectfully, David returned it to the briefcase, took out his pen and notepad, and began to ask questions about Assad's childhood in Damascus and graduate studies in London. The president saw immediately that David was having a hard time writing quickly enough to keep up with the conversation, and he approved use of the tape recorder,

David Lesch interviewing Bashar al-Assad, 2004

even helping his interviewer prop it up with books to best secure the microphone and capture the conversation.

David and the translator were seated across from the president in comfortable chairs inlaid with small mother-of-pearl mosaics, typical in Middle Eastern furniture. A wooden coffee table—also inlaid with mosaics—separated the chairs, and an office desk with a few stacks of paper neatly organized stood on the far side of the room. A large painting behind the desk, chosen by Bashar's father, dominated the wall. It was a classic portrait of Salah ad-Din Yusuf ibn Ayyub (Saladin) on his horse, a tribute to a heroic figure in Middle Eastern history who was known for his exploits, especially the liberation of Jerusalem from the Christian Crusaders in the twelfth century, and was admired for unifying the Islamic world against the invaders. David surmised it was a not-so-subtle reference to Hafez's struggles with Israel.

For the next two weeks, the interviews occurred almost every morning. Topics ranged from the Assad family's Alawite roots to the president's older brother Bassel's death in 1994. The two men talked openly about their shared experience of unexpected career paths. Bashar knew that an injury had caused David to abandon a promising future as a major league baseball player, and David knew the history of Bashar's decision to leave his chosen field of ophthalmology to assume his new role as eldest son and successor to his father's legacy. They discussed the cultural underpinnings of Bashar's decision, and David was surprised when the president described some of the emotional aspects that surrounded his choice.

According to Bashar, in contrast to stories circulating in the West, his father was originally against his son's plan to abandon medicine. Apparently it took weeks for Bashar to convince him that he wanted to remain in Syria, but once Hafez reluctantly accepted the idea, he began to build his son's legitimacy and power base within the Ba'ath Party with his usual force. Pictures began to appear all over the country of Hafez, Bassel, and Bashar together, with the inscription "the Leader, the Example, and the Hope." Almost immediately Bashar was appointed chair of the Syrian Computer Society, charged with overhauling the country's old-fashioned technology systems. It was a task he relished as a self-declared computer nerd. At the group's first meeting, Bashar clicked the keys on his laptop to display the website for the White House in Washington, demonstrating immediate access to information half a world away and erasing any doubts that internet technology was the way of the future.

He was also fast-tracked through the ranks of the military, reaching the equivalent of brigadier general in a few short years. In October 1998 his father called him into the president's office in the Rowda Building. Hafez's most trusted advisers—Mustafa Tlass, the minister of defense; Farouk al-Sharaa, the minister of foreign affairs; and Vice President Abdul Halim Khaddam—were already in the room. This was obviously an important meeting.

Hafez got down to business immediately and announced that he was turning over "the Lebanon file" to his son. Only the vice president voiced hesitation. That responsibility had been his for years and he was reluctant to give it up. Bashar watched as the others in the room let Khaddam know there was no choice, and that the matter was settled. Once the other men left the room, Hafez warned his son that some government officials might not be as loyal as he thought, announcing that "if there are to be any changes in the future, these individuals must be removed."

In the months that followed Syrians saw some of those individuals confronted with ruthless precision. Various high-ranking military officers were imprisoned, and when Hafez's armed troopers stormed the office of the prime minister, he shot himself. These were dark stories that reached the international community, events that Bashar absorbed as he thought about his future as Hafez's successor. He did not have to wait long. Two years later his father died and Bashar became president of Syria. The world was watching to see how that country's next chapters would unfold.

In their interviews in the Rowda Building, Bashar touched briefly on his father's thirty-year presidency, but he focused more on his own plans to revitalize the country's disastrous economy and push developments in technology. His self-deprecating manner and occasional winsome laugh were appealing, and the stories he told about his childhood, meeting and marrying his wife, or something one of his young children had recently done created an immediate rapport.

The third of five children, Bashar told David that as a middle child he had to get along with all of his siblings, describing his childhood as "very normal" with "very caring parents," surrounded by friends who treated him "like any other guy" despite the fact that his father was the president. Bashar and his family still lived in the modest home where he had grown up. Impromptu neighborhood games of soccer still took place in the street in front of the building, although in 2004 David noticed that the entrance to the street was blocked off by security. He felt a kinship with Bashar when the president described how sports and family were intertwined in his life. "If you do not work out, you won't have the energy," Bashar explained. "Every other day I work out for a couple of hours in the morning, particularly on a stationary bike. I also make sure I see my family in the morning every day, and then I do my work...and I make sure I see my family in the evening. If I have to work late, I go home early to see my children before they go to bed and then I go back to my office."

In 2005 musician Jeff Lynne, the founder of Electric Light Orchestra, contacted David. In addition to producing classic songs like "Don't Bring Me Down" and "Evil Woman" with ELO, in the 1990s he helped form the Traveling Wilburys, a supergroup that at first kept its members' names a secret. They were some of the most famous musicians of the time—George Harrison, Bob Dylan, Roy Orbison, and Tom Petty—and the music world went wild when their identities were revealed. When Lynne learned that Bashar was a fan of ELO, he sent David a handwritten note, along with a package of CDs, to present as a gift to the Syrian president. It was a unique approach to diplomacy, and it was well received by Assad.

David's interviews with some of Bashar's childhood friends confirmed his focus on family and athletics and noted his non-confrontational personality, especially when compared to his father, who was known for his authoritative leadership style. But David would later write the following: "Officials and commentators in the West failed to grasp that Bashar is profoundly Syrian—he had only spent eighteen months of his life in London, and they were not during the formative years of his life. He is the son of Hafez al-Assad, a child of the Arab-Israeli conflict and the Cold War, the keeper of the Alawite flame. While his hobbies include Western technology and music, and his family life appears quite modern, maintaining Syria's traditional interests has always been his obligation."

The hard realities were that Bashar had inherited an authoritarian state from his father, with a stagnant economy, pervasive corruption, and political repression. Like several other countries in the Middle East, it was a mukhabarat state—one in which the security or intelligence services, along with certain trusted elements in the military, are dominant in controlling the population. Hafez had created a tangled matrix of overlapping security agencies during his time in power. With its history of political upheaval, most of the Syrian population willingly accepted less freedom in exchange for more stability. Since the early 1970s Syria had been able to "straddle the fence" regionally and internationally. On the one hand, it was the cradle of Arab nationalism, in the forefront of the states arrayed against Israel, and supportive of groups like Hezbollah and Hamas. On the other hand, it sent troops to support the US-led United Nations forces that evicted Iraq from Kuwait in the 1991 Gulf War.

In the early years of Bashar's presidency, his increased verbal attacks on Israel and support for Hamas/Hezbollah fueled fears within an ascendant group of US foreign-policy experts who pushed for closer scrutiny of Syria. Not long before David arrived in Damascus for his first interviews, President Bush announced that "Syria must choose the right side in the war on terror by closing terrorist camps and expelling terrorist organizations." David knew that Syria assumed that the clear differences between al-Qaeda and Hamas/Hezbollah were self-evident. He also knew that the more subtle distinctions were lost on the Bush administration and that this misunderstanding would lead to trouble. When David asked Bashar about the growing rift between Syria and the United States, he replied, "Some see me as bad, some as good—we don't actually care what terms they use. It is not right to apply this term to Syria—I mean, look at the relationship Syria has with the rest of the world; if you have good relations with the rest of the world, you are not a rogue state just because the United States says you are."

Through the Syrian lens, the US invasion of Iraq in 2003 meant that 150,000 American troops were suddenly on its eastern border. To the north was Turkey, a member of NATO; to the south were Israel and Jordan, both strong allies of the United States. Syria was in a precarious position, and Bashar had to tread carefully in the early years of his presidency. Under pressure from the United States to do more about Syrian insurgents crossing into Iraq, he chose to appeal to Arab nationalism instead, strengthening his own support base. David understood that with chaos reigning in Iraq and instability growing in Lebanon, it was not hard for Bashar to remind the Syrian populace that US-promoted democracy could rip the fabric of society apart, even its own. David wrote that "weathering these multiple storms took a great deal of ability—with a bit of luck thrown in. Bashar al-Assad was no longer the untested, inexperienced leader. No one remains president of Syria very long without being capable and cunning."

Growing worries in Washington about Bashar's negative reaction to the Bush Doctrine led to a spate of harsh congressional testimony, covered in detail in David's 2012 book, *Syria: The Fall of the House of Assad*. Eliot Engel, a Democratic representative from New York, asserted, "We will not tolerate Syrian support for terrorism. We will not tolerate Syrian occupation of Lebanon....I do not want to witness horrors worse than 9/11." The negative sentiments were bipartisan. Dick Armey, a Republican

Downtown Damascus, Syria, circa 2004

representative from Texas, testified, "Our inaction on holding Syria accountable for its dangerous activities could seriously diminish our efforts on the war on terrorism and brokering a viable peace in the Middle East." And comments from Shelley Berkley, a Democratic representative from Nevada, were aimed directly at Syria's president: "I don't care if he's a doctor, a lawyer, a plumber, or a carpenter—this is not a kinder, gentler leader. This is a kinder and gentler terrorist, and we don't need another one of those."

As David continued to question Bashar and record his responses, he was acutely aware of the complexity of the story he planned to tell. Despite Washington's growing concern about Syria and its leader, David's long conversations, covering both controversial issues and personal experiences, presented a more nuanced picture of a young leader in one of the most conflicted regions in the world. Bashar shared his frustration at having signed a hundred new decrees, with only a handful reaching implementation. The country's labyrinth of bureaucratic positions that slowed all progress had forced the president to resort to negotiating and manipulating to get anything done. He reminisced with David about how different his career as an eye surgeon had been, when a simple procedure produced immediate results for his patient. The arena of politics, Syrian style, was much less clear. David listened with an open mind, recorded Bashar's responses, and delved deeper into the issues that would eventually fill the pages of *The New Lion of Damascus*.

The Assad family's residential palace was nestled in the foothills of Mount Qasioun, which overlooked the city, a twenty-minute journey from Bashar's office. Early one morning the official motorcade picked up David at the hotel and drove toward the foothills and the sacred mountain beyond, the repository of so many stories from the past. The landscape changed as they left the bustling streets of modern Damascus, sped through the old walled city, and entered the vast desert. David was momentarily transported to the ancient past as his car traveled up a road on the mountain where the Prophet Abraham was born, according to the twelfth-century Islamic scholar Ibn Asakir. The Quran says that Abraham witnessed the stars and the moon, and eventually sunrise, for the first time on the mountain, "experiencing the wonders of the heavens and the Earth" that instilled in him an everlasting faith. The legendary "Cave of Blood" (Magharat al-Dam) was much farther up the slope, the site where Cain supposedly killed his brother Abel, a deed that would be described in medieval Arab history books as the world's first murder.

But when David arrived at the family compound, all thoughts of the past were forgotten when he saw the beautiful First Lady of Syria standing on the steps to greet him. Asma Akhras al-Assad was born in 1975 in London. Her father was a cardiologist who worked at the Cromwell Hospital, and her mother served as first secretary at the Syrian embassy. They were Sunni Muslims who spoke Arabic at home and often spent holidays with family in Syria but also embraced their British life. Asma was known as "Emma" in her local Church of England primary school, and as a teenager she attended a private girls' school near her father's Harley Street office. After graduating from Kings College with a degree in computer science, she went to work as a banker at J.P. Morgan in New York. She had just been admitted to an MBA program at Harvard University when she began dating an eye doctor named Bashar al-Assad, who happened to be the son of Syria's president. They married in 2000, shortly after Bashar assumed the presidency, and their first child, Hafez, was born the following year.

Standing on the steps of her luxurious home in the shadows of Mount Qasioun, Asma was tall and thin, elegantly dressed in a silk suit, with understated jewelry. She led David into her office for what was scheduled as an hour-long interview. He noticed the large mirror on the wall behind her, no doubt a two-way security fixture, and smiled at whoever might be watching. She began the conversation with two direct questions: Why was David interested in her husband, and why did he want to write a book about him? He was surprised by her bluntness and responded by telling her that he identified with Bashar's unexpected path to the presidency. He shared his own shift in careers from baseball to academics and told her he wanted to explore how her husband felt about leaving medicine behind to lead Syria, and how he intended to guide his country's future.

She told David that one of the things that attracted her to Bashar was that he always tried to see the best in every situation, and that "he is always thinking and wants to know what every

David Lesch with Syrian First Lady Asma al-Assad, 2004

Syrian is thinking." She described what it was like to ride in the car with her husband, his reaction to the people he saw along the roads, going about their daily activities. She said he wondered aloud what each of them wanted or needed.

Three hours later David was still there, listening to stories about her past life in London, her difficult relationship with her powerful mother-in-law, and her hopes for Syria's future. She had drawn up plans to establish a nonprofit called Massar, which would engage the country's youth in "active citizenship," and for an NGO that would serve as a rural microcredit association for young people trying to develop business skills. As she raised her arms to emphasize a point about her strong support of women's rights, her blouse lifted slightly. David noticed that her belly button was pierced with a diamond charm. Asma was a captivating figure indeed. A reporter for *Paris Match* called her "the element

Bashar and Asma al-Assad with their oldest son, Hafez, circa 2004

of light in a country of shadow zones," clearly struck by the First Lady's unique combination of intelligence and glamour, while also recognizing the darker situation in Syria that would come into full international view in the years ahead.

While her office was contemporary in style, with modern furniture, light wood floors, and glass top tables, the rest of the palace was more traditional. As Asma led David through various rooms, she showed him art from several well-known galleries in Paris, beautiful French antiques comingled with typical Middle East furniture inlaid with mother-of-pearl, and, of course, exquisite Persian rugs from neighboring Iran. On that first visit David also noticed a plethora of children's toys strewn across those rugs, reminding him of when Michael was a toddler fascinated by action figures and miniature trucks. He was touched by the simple realization that there is common ground wherever children play, regardless of nationality or religion. His Holiness the Dalai Lama summed it up succinctly in his book about happiness: "If you watch children playing together, they don't ask each other about their background, race, or beliefs; they simply recognize others like themselves, smile, and play together. I believe that we as human beings of all seven billion of us are the same. The way we are born and the way we die is the same; the way we eat, sleep, and dream is the same. As human beings we are the same, and this is something we need to think more about."

That philosophy had long been at the heart of David's worldview, and common ground was familiar turf in his life. In team sports, finding it had led to championships. In academics it led to promotions, awards, and the satisfaction of seeing education transform students' lives. And in conflict resolution, David recognized it as the only place to start. From the baseball diamond to Trinity's history department, from the presidential palace in Damascus to hostage negotiations in the decades to come, David made it his trademark. The results have been powerful and transformative. It is understandable that he sought to find traits in Bashar that might produce a positive dialogue for the future. He believed that he had done so, and like the rest of the world, he was disappointed when Syria's president began to follow a different path not long after *The New Lion of Damascus* was published in 2005.

The book was not an international bestseller, but sales were robust and government agencies and NGOs working in the Middle East recognized that it gave the Western world a firsthand, behind-the-scenes introduction to the Syrian president that no diplomatic briefings could produce. And because David had developed a good rapport with Bashar al-Assad, the men continued to meet frequently over the next few years. He was in Syria in early 2005 when Rafiq Hariri, the billionaire businessman and former Lebanese prime minister, was assassinated by a car bomb in Beirut. The international community immediately held Syria at least indirectly responsible for the killing. The US ambassador to Syria was recalled the day after the event, and the UN investigation of the assassination implicated Syrian officials close to Bashar, including his brother Maher al-Assad, commander of the Republican Guard, and his brother-in-law Assef Shawkat, head of Syrian intelligence, in its preliminary report.

In the aftermath of the assassination, Western countries and most of the Arab world were united in calling for the withdrawal of Syria's more than fourteen thousand troops from Lebanon. Since coming to power in 2000, Bashar already had reduced Syria's troop presence by 50 percent. Now he had to respond to regional and international pressure to complete a total withdrawal by April. During meetings in Damascus with Bashar that year, David saw a change in the Syrian president. He was defensive and angry, and he felt insulted that he had received little credit from the West for his compliance with its demands for withdrawal from Lebanon.

As the year progressed, Bashar used the political fallout from "losing Lebanon" to push aside internal domestic problems and consolidate his power. Abdul Halim Khaddam, the country's vice president who had dared to question Hafez al-Assad's decision to fast-track Bashar to power, was not part of the new president's inner circle and was one of the first officials forced to resign. In early 2006 Bashar began to feel a little more secure and sure of his future. David visited Syria twice that year, shortly after the shake-up in Bashar's cabinet and again as the 2006 Lebanon War was occurring in the summer. Bashar's position in the region improved still more. Israel was unable to defeat Hezbollah and withdrew most troops in October, and a victory for Hezbollah was a victory for Syria.

David Lesch with Pakistan's prime minister Benazir Bhutto, 2006

In March of 2006 David had given a talk at the Center for Strategic and International Studies (CSIS) in Washington, DC. At the time he was advocating the importance of establishing dialogue with Syria and its president. After the program a senior policy adviser on Vice President Dick Cheney's staff approached him. He expressed agreement with most of David's insights, then suddenly bellowed, "But those sons of bitches are killing our boys in Iraq!" In that moment David realized the immensity of the emotional component associated with the issues and knew it must be factored into the US-Syria dynamic before any diplomatic relationship could be built.

He told Cheney's staffer that he regularly volunteered at the world-famous burn unit at Brooke Army Medical Center in San Antonio, where many US soldiers wounded in the Iraq War were being treated. Images of his parents' terrible burns flashed through his mind, along with the knowledge that some of the horrific explosive devices in use and suicide bombings taking place in the Iraq War were perhaps facilitated by the very man he

David Lesch in Damascus after Bashar al-Assad's reelection, 2007

had been meeting regularly in Damascus. And yes, he was angry. But he also suggested that administration officials needed to do some role-playing, to view the world through the same lens as Damascus. His opinion pieces for the *Washington Post*, the *New York Times*, and other newspapers and magazines carried the message that Syria "needed to be invited into the diplomatic circle," noting that "Bashar al-Assad is sticking around."

These were remarkable years to be taking David's courses at Trinity, and his students recognized that they were watching history unfold, assessed and explained by an insightful professor who was at the heart of the action. In 2006 former Pakistani prime minister Benazir Bhutto, a fellow Harvard graduate, spoke to David's class. She was lovely and brilliant. When she was violently assassinated a year later following a public speech in Punjab, David's students felt a sense of personal loss and the profound reality of the chaos in the Middle East.

David returned to Damascus in 2007 in time to witness the resounding reelection of Bashar as Syria's president. Crowds in the streets seemed jubilant about the results of the unopposed election. David met with Bashar the day of the election, and he witnessed a change in the Syrian president. Bashar exhibited both exhilaration and relief, confiding to David that he had not been certain his popularity was so strong and vowing to build on his country's mandate. David asked Bashar what he thought of the overwhelming election victory, expecting the president to downplay it because it was a foregone conclusion. Instead Bashar said of the Syrian people, "they love me." In that moment David realized Bashar "had drunk the Kool-Aid of power" and planned to be president for life. An important and ominous shift in the Syrian story had taken place. He congratulated the president but had mixed feelings about what this growing empowerment might mean in the years ahead.

As word spread in US government agencies and think tanks that David had direct access to Syria's president, he became an unofficial liaison between Syria and the United States. He testified in front of the US Senate Committee on Foreign Relations in November 2007, recommending that the US reengage with Syria. The committee's chair, Senator Joe Biden, was traveling, and Senator John Kerry chaired the session. A few days later David wrote to Bashar that Kerry had agreed and that efforts were underway to issue an official invitation for Bashar to attend an international conference that was in the planning stages. The letter went on to suggest ideas about other topics he and Bashar had discussed, reflecting David's inclusion in the Syrian president's inner circle, and outlined his plans to visit Damascus early in 2008.

During the 1970s and 1980s Joanne King Herring, a socialite and political activist from Houston, became part of the inner circle of another Middle East country. She was a longtime friend of Pakistan's former president, Muhammad Zia-ul-Haq, and had

IN THE LION'S DEN

a close relationship with US Congressman Charlie Wilson, who was working on ways to end the fighting in Afghanistan. Wilson and Herring worked together on several peace-building projects, and their efforts became the plot of a 2003 book and a 2007 film, *Charlie Wilson's War*, starring Tom Hanks as Wilson and Julia Roberts as Herring. With new plans to produce a documentary film about the region she loved, Herring asked her creative team to contact David about possibly narrating the project. But before stardom became a reality, he learned that Herring had chosen actor Sean Connery instead. David considers it the best rejection letter he ever received.

It was shortly followed by a new possibility for positive action in the Middle East, making it easy to leave dreams of Hollywood behind. A friend at Harvard's Program on Negotiation (PON) proposed that his unique access to Bashar could help promote an innovative idea to build understanding between the West and the Middle East. To find out more, David would need to travel to Boulder, Colorado, and take a long walk around a beautiful lake.

Maaloula, Syria, an ancient town considered for the Abraham Path Initiative walking trail

THE PATH OF ABRAHAM

"You must meet William Ury," Joshua Weiss told David during a meeting at Trinity University. "He is working on something important and far-reaching, and Syria's participation is essential to its success. We think you could be really helpful."

David was familiar with Ury's decades-long career in mediation and with Harvard Law School's Program on Negotiation, where Weiss served as director. Weiss told him that, for the past five years, Ury had been committed to a new approach to building bonds between the Middle East and the rest of the world. Stephanie Saldaña, a colleague of both men, had read *The New Lion of Damascus* and suggested there could be exciting synergy to explore. The project, called the Abraham Path Initiative, was envisioned as a 1,200-mile walking trail across the Middle East designed to foster global understanding. David's deep knowledge of the region, with its diverse cultures and landscapes, would be an asset to the project, and his direct connection to Syria's president was incredibly valuable. Intrigued, he flew from San Antonio to Boulder in April 2007 to meet Ury in person and to learn more.

"Let's take a walk," Ury suggested, with a twinkle in his eyes, pointing to a lake just beyond his house. As a tangerine-colored sunset settled over lime-green aspen trees, the two men strolled. Ury told David that shortly after the terror attacks on 9/11, he had walked around the lake on a starry night with friends who had just returned from Syria. Wars were raging in the Middle East, and Americans were reeling from the violence they had witnessed on US soil. They wondered what they could do.

"And that is where the idea of the path was born, right here on this lake," he said. Dressed in his usual professorial attire, David knew his oxford loafers would soon be caked in mud, but he was certain that the walk, and the ideas he was about to discuss, were worth a new pair of shoes. William Ury had cofounded the Harvard Negotiation Project (HNP) with Roger Fisher in 1979 and served as a mediator in the Balkans, South America, Africa, the Soviet Union, and the Middle East. Working with former president Jimmy Carter, he established an NGO dedicated to ending civil wars around the world, and his bestselling book about conflict, *Getting to Yes: Getting to Agreement Without Giving In*, cowritten with Fisher, sold more than 15 million copies and was translated into more than thirty-five languages.

A life-changing adventure when he was six years old may have been the spark that fueled Ury's journey into the complex world of conflict resolution. His mother wanted to move the family from Midwest America to Switzerland in 1959. Her lifelong dream had been to live in Europe for a year. Ury's father was not so keen on the idea. Their discussions were sometimes heated, but they reached consensus. The outcome was exposure to a very different multicultural world, with mountain landscapes, new languages, and local memories of the devastation of World War II in Europe still lingering. Along with that expanded worldview came the exciting realization that there are many doors to open and ideas to understand.

Like Dorothy in *The Wizard of Oz*, Ury says he knew immediately

THE PATH OF ABRAHAM   137

that he "wasn't in Kansas anymore." He embraced the adventure and never looked back, eventually earning a degree from Yale University in anthropology and a doctorate from Harvard. On a cold evening in 1977 Ury was working on his dissertation paper when the telephone rang late at night. It was Roger Fisher, one of his Harvard professors, calling to tell him that he had liked Ury's paper on the anthropological perspective in the Middle East and that he had sent it to a colleague in the State Department who was working on peace negotiations. "I was thunderstruck," Ury says, "that an idea I had in my little rented attic room might actually be of practical help. And that's what really plunged me from academic anthropology into a kind of applied anthropology—combining mediation and negotiation and, of course, listening." It is something he has done all over the world.

In his more than ten books, Ury always circles back to the art of listening as a crucial skill when dealing with conflict. His observation that conflict is an integral part of the human experience—from mild family disagreements about what's for dinner, to dramas in corporate board rooms, to countries firing missiles at their perceived enemies—is strangely reassuring. It is to be expected, and it can be resolved. As the two scholars strolled around the lake in 2007, the conversations between Ury and David were meaningful on both a global and personal level. On the home front, David was experiencing problems in his twenty-one-year marriage to Suzanne. With his frequent travel to places far beyond Texas, they had grown apart and had decided to separate. His conversation with Ury provided a helpful frame of reference to navigate his marital circumstances, and tackling international stumbling blocks in familiar Syrian territory was an intriguing challenge.

Ury explained that the idea of the Abraham Path Initiative (API) was born in 2003, the result of a walk around the lake with

Elias Amidon, the spiritual director of the Sufi Way. When Amidon traveled to Syria later that year, he met with colleague and friend Father Paolo Dall'Oglio, an Italian Jesuit priest, to talk about ways to improve Muslim-Christian understanding. The abbot of Deir Mar Musa al-Habashi, a monastery located about fifty miles from Damascus, Father Paolo had convinced another important player to join them. The Grand Mufti of Syria, Shaykh Ahmed Kuftaro, liked what he heard, and the three men—a Sufi, a Christian, and a Muslim—began to envision a walking trail through the Middle East. It was a bold plan. Could it possibly become a road to peace, something that had proved elusive for centuries?

"To solve a problem, walk around," Ury said to David with a smile, crediting author Gregory McNamee's translation of St. Jerome, a simple but profound instruction he kept framed on his desk in Colorado. He smiled again, a trademark immediately putting his listener at ease, and added, "I love to walk—it is the very essence of transformation." David's thoughts flashed back to the months he spent exploring London, Paris, Damascus, and the smaller towns in Syria on foot while researching his dissertation. He told Ury the concept resonated with him and quickly agreed to join the project.

The API already had formed a host committee, created its organizational structure, and raised funds to move forward by the time David came on board as a consultant. A delegation had visited Turkey, Syria, Lebanon, Jordan, Israel, and Palestine to introduce the project to government and religious leaders and to explore how mapping the proposed walking trail could occur collaboratively. Like the Camino de Santiago pilgrimage route in Spain and Portugal, the Abraham Path would link historic sites and holy places, breaking down cultural barriers in what journalist Christiane Amanpour called "the most divided region in the world." The path was named for Abraham (Ibrahim), the legendary "messenger of God" who is so important to Islam, Judaism, and Christianity and recognized as an ancestor of Muhammad, Moses, and Jesus. Stories of his travels across the Middle East on foot nearly 4,500 years ago appear in the Quran and the Hebrew and Christian Bibles. The proposed walking trail would initially trace Abraham's ancient journeys across those six countries, with plans to eventually include Iraq, Egypt, and Saudi Arabia.

Aware that Syria's participation was essential to the first phase of the walking trail, and having encountered troublesome roadblocks from that government, Ury asked David to be a twenty-first-century messenger, carrying the project proposal directly to Bashar al-Assad in Damascus. "With all that is going on in the Middle East," he says, "we have designed a project that carries a banner of optimism. Sometimes it seems like we are tilting at windmills, and David is a natural at that. We have tilted at those windmills together, and he never loses sight of the history and culture of the region. He has an empathetic lens. He is not quick to judge. He tries to understand things from within. He is a listener, and he remains undaunted."

All those qualities were needed when David carried the API's message to Syria in May 2007. The country's minister of tourism, Saadallah Agha al-Qalaa, had already offered the cooperation of his agency to Ury's group but was concerned that Israel might use the project to further its agenda. The fact that the Abraham Path would geographically link Syria with Israel indirectly through Jordan, with the two countries still officially at war and diplomatically jostling over the Golan Heights, caused concern among Syrian officials. David was charged with arranging to meet with Bashar to be sure the president was aware of the project and to describe its potential economic benefits and the likelihood of an improved image for Syria in the West.

As David entered the now familiar Rowda Building in Damascus and took the stairs to the second floor, he looked forward to his reunion with the Syrian president. Surprisingly, Bashar did not appear to know about the project, which raised some concerns about his security establishment and why it had not informed him. But he seemed enthusiastic about the concept and promised to meet with the API delegation next time it visited the country. He had one caveat: the project and its implementation in Syria would need support from the country's Sunni religious leaders. Bashar agreed to openly back it if the planners could obtain the blessing of that majority, including the new Grand Mufti, who was a close friend of Ghias Barakat from their days in Aleppo. The president suggested that David communicate with an array of religious and business leaders who might be willing to help move that process forward, and meetings were scheduled over his next few days in Syria. But there was no mention of needing to win the support of the mukhabarat, the country's security apparatus.

The director of the Islamic Studies Center in Damascus was quick to see the value of the project, and he introduced David to Samir (fictional name), one of the country's leading businessmen, who became the project's biggest supporter at the time. Through his assistance, David met with a top Sufi imam and more than twenty Sunni imams. They shared prayers and meals, and frank conversations about the project ensued. Discussions shifted to Israel and the Golan Heights, considered by Syrians to be their land and unlawfully occupied by Israel since the 1967 Arab-Israeli war.

The dialogue grew heated and emotional, but David was prepared and had the perfect response ready. He told the gathering that the Palestinians had already signed up as supporters of the project and were actively participating in it. With the approval of the Palestinian Authority, a tour-operating group had mapped out and opened a segment of the path in the West Bank. He showed them some brochures advertising the walking trail in Palestine. The imams and businessmen at the dinner overwhelmingly gave their consent to the plan and promised to do what they could to help. Other factions, however, were busy with their own negative counterplans. During David's meeting at a religious center earlier that day, photos were taken of him with the imams. They appeared over the next few days in state-controlled newspapers along with stories about the meetings and the Abraham Path. One headline read "The Abraham Path (Upon Him Peace): A Big International Project or a Dangerous Jewish Pilgrimage?" The coverage resulted in intensified efforts by the mukhabarat to thwart the project. When David returned to the United States, he cautioned the API team to travel to Damascus as soon as possible to help solidify the support he had begun to build and before military intelligence officials escalated their opposition.

Although Bashar was not available during the next trip in June 2007, the organization's representatives, which included David, William Ury, cofounder Elias Amidon, executive director Tyler Norris, and the head of trail development Dan Adamson, met with several leading government officials and were entertained by a growing number of business leaders. David's contact Samir hosted an elaborate dinner at his villa south of Damascus, attended by several important imams. Just before the meal began, the head imam asked David to lead the prayers. Caught off guard, he briefly felt panic, but he called on his Catholic school upbringing to recite something resembling the Beatitudes, the blessings delivered by Jesus of Nazareth in his Sermon on the Mount. Impressed by David's ability to rise to the occasion, Ury leaned over to whisper how wonderful the prayer had been and to ask how he had come up with it. Always the historian, David laughingly told him that his words were not original source material.

The group also met for another dinner with General Manaf Tlass and his wife at a well-known restaurant in the old city of Damascus. Tlass was a close friend of Bashar's and commander of the elite fourth armored division, effectively the military protector of the government. David knew him quite well from previous visits, and as a historian he knew that Tlass's father, Mustsafa, had been the longest-serving minister of defense under Hafez al-Assad and one of the most powerful men in Syria. The dinner seemed a good omen for the project, and a special luncheon the next day was another sign that things were going well. Ghias Barakat, the minister of education and David's long-time friend who had first approached Bashar about *The New Lion of Damascus*, invited the API members to join several important ministers, including Bouthaina Shaaban and Faisal Mekdad, the deputy foreign minister, at an elegant restaurant nestled on the side of Mount Qasioun.

Barakat's driver noticed that a car with two mukhabarat was following them. The minister remarked that it was very strange and later during the meal warned David, "Be careful; those guys are in the restaurant's kitchen." No doubt some of the waiters were on the payroll of the secret security force. A few hours later David realized he had been poisoned to prevent his participation in an important meeting later in the day with the Grand Mufti. He was dizzy and nauseous and startled by the intensity of his sudden headache. He somehow made it through that meeting, and the Grand Mufti indicated his initial approval of the project.

"Abraham is our common father," the religious leader said, "and we are all part of only one religion, the religion of Ibra-him and that spirit of hospitality and kindness that he evokes and represents." David was not so sure about the hospitality or kindness as he stumbled into the elevator following the meeting. He collapsed, and his colleagues helped him into a taxi, assuming he was suffering from food poisoning. The next day he was still ill and unable to depart with the rest of the delegation. He flew home a few days later, and Ury thanked him for his "heroic diplomacy." It would not be the last time this advocate for the Abraham Path Initiative felt the dangerous reach of the mukhabarat in Syria.

Ury and the rest of the API group returned to the United States in a positive state of mind, believing they had the support of the Syrian government and unaware that David had been intentionally poisoned. Plans were made to return to Syria in a month to develop the first segment of the path in collaboration with the Ministry of Tourism. But other forces were also at work, and despite the Grand Mufti's tacit approval and support from Syrian business leaders, the project was perceived by some as anti-Islamist. The Grand Mufti of Jordan refused to endorse it, and there were concerns that it might somehow be confused with or compete with Hajj, the annual Islamic pilgrimage to Mecca. When several members of the project-planning group attempted to return to Damascus in the fall, they were denied visas by the Syrian embassy in Washington. David contacted his good friend Imad Moustapha to find out why. The ambassador explained that the applicants had previously visited "Occupied Palestine" (Israel), so they were not wanted in Syria. He suggested that David call on Bashar directly to get the project back on track.

In early November David arrived in Damascus with a confirmed meeting with Bashar scheduled for the next morning. But no official cars waited on the tarmac at the airport, and no one from the president's office was there to shepherd him through customs. David handed his passport to the agent, and the officer picked up the telephone. After a brief pause, he told David he was on the blacklist of undesirables who should not be let into the country. Suddenly a group of officers from Syrian Air Force intelligence collected him and his luggage and took him down a long corridor to a small, windowless room. David's heart pounded. He knew he was about to be interrogated. He was not terribly worried, having gone through the same process in other Arab countries over the years. If things did not go well, he assumed he would be put on the next plane departing the country, no matter the destination.

His chair was positioned lower than the others, requiring him to look up at the officers about to question him. They sat in total silence for a while, a ploy certainly meant to evoke fear. David called on the calm he had always displayed on the pitcher's mound. A colonel finally entered the room, pulled out his pistol, and spun it menacingly on a coffee table between them. For the next three hours David answered the same question: "Why are you in Syria?" He repeatedly told the interrogator that he had an appointment with the president the next morning, and he handed the officer a card with the name and phone number of the protocol officer at the Rowda Building. Eventually the colonel picked up the telephone and dialed the number.

David still recalls the terrified look on the colonel's face. The protocol officer confirmed that he was an author who had written a book about Bashar and that he was scheduled to see the president the next day. The colonel was appropriately remorseful, then asked David for an autograph. He had a pen but no paper, so he asked David to sign the back of the blacklist that had caused all the trouble in the first place. Then he instructed the security officers to provide David with a VIP escort to the Sheraton Hotel.

The episode was troubling for a variety of reasons beyond the interrogation. David had a visa that had been stamped at the Syrian embassy in Washington when he met with the ambassador,

THE PATH OF ABRAHAM 145

and he was well known in Syria as an American scholar who frequently met with Bashar. He was aware that he had been followed by the mukhabarat on previous visits, that a camera had been placed in his hotel room's air vent on at least one occasion, and that his telephone was most likely tapped during his visits. But the manner of interrogation seemed different and more ominous. When he met with the president the next morning, Bashar asked how his flight and arrival in Damascus had been. David told him about the incident at the airport, and the president seemed genuinely surprised and apologetic. He immediately called some staff members into the office and ordered them to find out what had happened, reassuring David that it would never occur again.

"Mr. President," David said slowly, "if you do not control these guys, I am afraid they will come back and haunt you." The observation would prove true in 2011 when the catalyst for Syria's participation in the Arab Spring was an event initiated by the mukhabarat without the president's approval. The rest of the meeting was cordial, and both men acknowledged the obstacles that the Abraham Path was facing. Bashar suggested changing the name of the path in Syria to something that carried less religious volatility and did not include "Abraham" in the title, explaining that sometimes manipulating the process was the only way to get something done in his country. The president indicated that he was not ready to publicly champion the path in Syria until the planners came up with a new name and garnered more local backing.

More intrigue arose a few days later, when Samir called David to cancel the dinner party at his villa that night, explaining that "something had come up." Later that evening, as David packed his bag for his return to the United States, a cryptic note was slipped under his hotel room door. It was from Samir and read "the right hand is preventing me from seeing you." David understood the message immediately. When he had described his airport ordeal to Samir a few days after he arrived, the businessman had said, "the right hand of security often does not know what the left hand of the presidency is doing—and vice versa." He later learned that General Assef Shawkat, the powerful head of Syrian military intelligence and Bashar's brother-in-law, had visited Samir's apartment in Damascus to advise him against seeing David again.

The Abraham Path Initiative gathered its partners and staff, including those working in the targeted areas of the Middle East, in Istanbul in late 2007. They discussed Bashar's idea of a name change for the Syrian segment of the path, eventually settling on the Syrian Cultural Walking Trail. It was neutral yet descriptive, and the team hoped it was innocuous enough to win approval at a meeting scheduled in Damascus early the next year.

On his way back to San Antonio to resume his teaching schedule at Trinity, David stopped in Washington to testify about US-Syria relations in front of the Senate Committee on Foreign Relations. Senator John Kerry presided, sitting in for the chair of the committee, Senator Joe Biden. Robert Malley from the International Crisis Group was another speaker. He would later become the director of Middle East affairs on the National Security Council and a lead negotiator for a US delegation that attempted to revive the nuclear deal with Iran in early 2020. When the session ended, a young man approached David with a handshake and a huge smile. He remembered taking David's seminar on the Middle East when he was a student at Trinity, and he told his former professor that the course had inspired him to pursue a career in government focusing on foreign policy issues. David felt a surge of pride as he chatted with his former student, who was now a senior staffer for one of the most important committees on the Hill. As he boarded his plane home, he thought about the

THE PATH OF ABRAHAM

students waiting for him in Texas, confident that some of them would also make important contributions to the world of international affairs someday.

In May 2008 Trinity University honored David for his outstanding scholarship. Various international think tanks and government agencies recognized his special expertise as well, and he was in high demand as a consultant on a myriad of issues related to Middle East policy. Oxford University Press published his book *The Arab-Israeli Conflict: A History*, and reviews in both academic journals and commercial media described it as one of the best books about the history of the Middle East, the Cold War, and US foreign policy.

That spring brought fulfillment into David's personal life as well. While playing tennis at The Club at Sonterra, he met a realtor named Judy Dunlap. They discovered a shared love for sports, international travel, intellectual pursuits, and eventually each other. Judy was born in Raleigh, North Carolina, was placed in a Jesuit orphanage by her biological parents, and was adopted when she was six months old. The family moved to New Jersey, where her father worked as an electrician and her mother drove a school van for children with special needs. Her parents always told her they had found the cutest baby in the orphanage, and when she was three or four years old, they asked if she would like a brother or sister. She told them she would rather have a puppy. Like David, Judy's childhood epitomized the idyllic American dream, and she did not want any unnecessary changes. She earned a degree in applied mathematics from North Carolina State University, combined her financial skills with a love of retail fashion and merchandising, and went to work for the Associated Dry Goods chain of department stores that owned Lord & Taylor in New York City, Robinson's of Florida, Goldwater's in Phoenix, and other stores around the United States. She also did private-label merchandising for Walmart and Target before moving from Seattle to San Antonio to help merchandise and market a line of clothing manufactured in Norway, intended to compete with The North Face label. "It became pretty obvious to me that ski apparel did not have a big future here," she explained with a laugh. In 1999 she made a major career shift.

Judy Urrutia, an interior designer, introduced her to Phyllis Browning, one of the city's top realtors, whose company would eventually become the largest independently owned brokerage in town, encompassing residential, commercial, and land and ranch real estate in Texas. In just a few short years Judy Dunlap became one of the company's top producers and remained with Phyllis Browning Company for more than twenty-five years. Like David, she had moved from one career path to another. She was undaunted by challenges, and she recognized the importance of teamwork—in a doubles match on the tennis court or when putting together a large real-estate sale.

David first spotted her on the tennis court at Sonterra. He was impressed by both her beauty and her competitiveness, and he attended a fancy dinner for members at the club, hoping to meet her. Halfway through the night she had not appeared, and David was disappointed. Suddenly he saw a woman's back, and a lovely dress—could it be Judy? When she turned and smiled at him, he felt the proverbial thunderbolt. They talked until the party ended but did not want to call it a night. They found a nearby wine bar and stayed until it closed. David, struck by their commonalities, decided it was destiny. Judy was a Jersey girl like his mother, she had been educated in the same part of the country he grew up in, and she loved sports. Except for her passion for the New York Yankees, instead of David's beloved Baltimore Orioles, they were in tune on every subject. As the evening drew to a close, Judy tilted her head to the side and smiled slightly. David felt something he had never experienced before—a warm shiver throughout his body. He was in love.

Complex teamwork involving David, William Ury, and the rest of the Abraham Path Initiative group dominated the summer months of 2008. Former president Jimmy Carter had formally endorsed the organization some years earlier, and it was well known that Bashar al-Assad admired Carter and the work of the Carter Center. Ury had a long history of working with Carter, and when he learned that the former president had scheduled a visit to Lebanon and Syria in December, he realized that the trip could push the walking trail dream forward in a big way. What if Carter and Bashar could be convinced to take a short walk together along an expected segment of the Syrian Cultural Walking Trail?

The Carter Center assigned Hrair Balian, the new director of its Conflict Resolution Program, to help coordinate the proposed walk. Balian grew up in Lebanon. His parents and grandparents had survived the genocide in Armenia between 1915 and 1920, and family discussions about the horrors of violent conflict were an important part of his childhood. He came to the United States in 1970 to pursue advanced studies and received his law degree from Golden Gate University in San Francisco. Before joining the Carter Center, he had worked for two decades with intergovernmental organizations including the United Nations and NGOs around the world, tackling issues ranging from human rights and elections to conflict resolution in the Balkans, Eastern Europe, independent states emerging from the former Soviet Union, the Middle East, and Africa.

The planners zeroed in on a notable short path in Maaloula, about thirty-four miles northwest of Damascus. The Christian Arab community of about three thousand people, mostly comprised of Greek Orthodox and Greek Catholics, is essentially built into the side of a mountain. The town had already been chosen as a site on the proposed walking trail and would be a perfect place for Carter and Bashar to walk together. David realized this could be the perfect opportunity to introduce Judy to the work that had become so important to him, and he invited her to join him on the adventure scheduled for the end of 2008. He could not wait to show her the ancient sites and modern developments in the country where he had spent so much time and energy. Michael, now eighteen years old, would accompany them.

David helped draft a letter that would be sent by Carter to Bashar explaining why the trail was significant from a geopolitical standpoint and pointing out that it would generate a more positive media image of Syria in the West and a better understanding of Syria's tolerance and religious diversity. Several members of the API team edited the letter, Carter made final tweaks, and it was sealed and sent to David, who would hand deliver it to Bashar when he visited Damascus in October. A tremendous amount of time went into planning the endeavor, and the team was asked to keep Carter's visit to the Middle East a secret until after the US presidential election in November. It was clear that the Democratic party did not want the visit to become a controversial issue or detrimental to the election outcome.

In early October David traveled to Damascus and met with Bashar for almost two hours. He handed the letter from Carter to the Syrian president, who said he had not heard about the proposed trip in December. But he seemed delighted with the news, telling David that he was "overwhelmingly positive" about the visit and that he would alter his schedule to meet with Carter. Then, on October 26, US special forces crossed into Syria from Iraq via helicopter. They conducted a military strike aimed at a foreign fighters' network, located near the border at Abu Kamal. The Syrian government called the raid a "criminal and terrorist attack" on its sovereignty. The incident added a new challenge to the evolving

Jimmy Carter and Bashar al-Assad in Damascus, 2008

plan for Carter to walk with Bashar in December, and other political and bureaucratic maneuvers added to this delicate dance of diplomacy. Both Bashar and Carter began to back away from the proposed walk in Maaloula, and the Syrian Cultural Walking Trail was moved to the bottom of the list of trip priorities.

David was later disappointed to learn that no one on the API team would be invited to participate in the events surrounding Carter's visit, but he understood the delicacy of the situation. He decided not to change his plans to travel to Syria with Judy and Michael and hoped that a last-minute invitation to be involved with the walk might be issued. They arrived in the country in December 2008. As in years past, officials from the president's office met the Lesch group with cars on the tarmac and took them to their hotel in VIP style. An intense and exhilarating tour of the country began. After one particularly busy day, David met friends at the bar at the Four Seasons Hotel, where the Carter entourage was staying.

David and Michael Lesch on Mount Qasioun overlooking Damascus, 2008

He saw Hrair Balian sitting alone and invited him to join his group. Over drinks—Johnny Walker black label double shots with ice—they shared dreams about conflict resolution in the Middle East, and Balian described how he had been interviewed to work at the Carter Center. The former president and his wife, Rosalynn, were sitting in a tandem double rocking chair, created by Carter in his own woodworking shop. They both asked Balian questions, evidence of their strong partnership that was witnessed by the world over the years. "Mr. Balian, what would you do for us in the Middle East?" the former president said. Balian smiled, flattered by this question from the man who had helped craft the Camp David Accords. He spotted a genuine collaborative spirit immediately, something he came to treasure over his years at the Carter Center. Balian would also enjoy important

Lesch family with hosts at Syrian villa party, 2008

collaboration with David in the future and friendship as well. But that night in the hotel bar both men were focused on the days ahead in Syria as the end of the year approached.

The Syrian president's office provided transportation, a full-time guide, and a security person for the Lesch family's five-day stay. They toured some of David's favorite sites, including Krak des Chevaliers and the magnificent Roman ruins at Palmyra. Their final night would be spectacular: a lavish farewell dinner hosted by David's acquaintance Samir, complete with music, Sufi dancers, and an exquisite meal. The trouble began in the desert oasis of Palmyra, once one of the most important cultural centers of the ancient world. Its ruins rose dramatically out of the desert. Stately sandstone columns, a grand colonnaded street with covered sides, and the great Temple of Baal conjured visions of wealthy caravans arriving there in the first century CE.

David had visited many times and had planned to share the UNESCO site's history with Judy and Michael, hoping to fascinate them with his stories. But he could not get out of the car. He waited while his family toured the ruins, feeling sicker by the minute. He remembered his earlier poisoning after the mukhabarat infiltrated a restaurant kitchen on Mount Qasioun. By the time the family was taken back to the hotel to change for the evening's festivities, David was certain he should not go to Samir's dinner. But when he called his host and learned of all the special arrangements that had been made, he summoned every bit of energy, took a deep breath, entered the car driven by one of Samir's sons with Judy and Michael, and headed into the desert.

Twinkling lights, Sufi dancers, music—including a three-part Arabic song that had been written about the Lesch family—and of course, an incredible feast, created a magical scene. For David, it was not unlike Alice in Wonderland's dizzying fall into that spectacular rabbit hole. What was real and what was imaginary? One minute he saw a whirling dervish dancing in the courtyard; the next moment he was pitching a baseball to Baltimore Oriole Hall of Famer Eddie Murray as a full stadium cheered him on. Judy was taken inside, where all the women were enjoying their tea, dressed traditionally, some with beautiful jewelry just barely visible. Since she did not speak Arabic and the women did not speak English, there was a lot of smiling and courteous nodding.

By now David was lying in a cabana in a small pavilion near the courtyard. Samir's personal doctor was on his way from Damascus. At last, he arrived with a special injection. He pulled down David's trousers, and an audience of men, women, and children stared as the doctor delivered the shot. At first Judy was fearful

Judy Dunlap and David Lesch married in 2009

that the injection might finish him off, something David was far beyond caring about at the time. But it worked, and miraculously he began to feel better. David, Judy, and Michael flew to Jordan the next morning, and at least for the moment, the Abraham Path Initiative's efforts in Syria appeared to have met with failure.

Fortunately, David and Judy's love story was well on its way to a happy ending. David was thrilled that the two women he adored most in the world could meet during the holidays in Baltimore. After seeing Judy and David so happy together, his mother Margaret announced, "I have my David back." She recognized that, after his unhappy marriage and divorce, her son had rediscovered that joyful spirit that had been absent for a while.

In March 2009 David and Judy traveled to Paris, and Judy was

Judy Dunlap and David Lesch in Paris, France

sure the trip would produce a marriage proposal. But David had not saved enough money to buy her the ring he wanted to give her: he was waiting for his tax refund. Judy was forced to wait another few months. He proposed in May, and the couple married at Bellagio in Las Vegas in August. Michael was their best man.

They spent their honeymoon in England and visited David's friend and mentor Sir Samuel Falle in his senior care facility in Bath on a rainy day. The diplomat told Judy that David should be awarded an endowed professorship at his university. A few years later his prediction came true.

David became Trinity University's Ewing Halsell Distinguished

Judy Dunlap and David Lesch with Sir Sam Falle, Bath, England, 2009

Professor of History. Teaching, highlighted by a classroom visit from Pervez Musharraf, the former president of Pakistan, international consultancies, and a newlywed partnership with the love of his life brought the decade to a very happy close. Impending events in the Middle East, however, would be a much different story.

Actress and former UN Refugee Agency special envoy Angelina Jolie at a Syrian refugee camp, 2010

DEATH AND DIPLOMACY

In 2010 Syria seemed to be a fairly stable place. President Bashar al-Assad and his wife Asma visited Paris in December and were photographed visiting museums and being hosted by the French elite. Asma was, as usual, elegantly dressed in haute couture, and Bashar smiled happily for the cameras. That same month the *Los Angeles Times* and the *New York Times* both published stories praising aspects of Syrian society, including its history and culture and the new directions of its government. Their headlines read "Syria a Bright Star in the Middle East" and "Preserving Heritage and the Fabric of Life in Syria." President Barack Obama's administration was attempting to restart the Syrian-Israeli peace negotiations, a process in which David was involved. Senator John Kerry had reportedly met Bashar five times in Damascus over a two-year period. David's insights about the Syrian president had helped set both the tone and expectations. Hollywood icons Brad Pitt and Angelina Jolie had visited refugee camps that Syria provided for displaced Iraqis and had dined with the country's First Family. All seemed well. And yet a year later the Center for the Study of Islam and Democracy in Washington, DC, sent an email to its leadership with a very different subject line: "ACT NOW to stop Bashar Assad's killing machine in Syria." As

Arab Spring protest in northwestern Syria, circa 2011

international media covered the growing protests in Syria, David was struck by how far Bashar had fallen in just twelve months.

The self-immolation of a young man in Tunisia in late 2010 prompted a series of protests and unrest, creating what came to be called the Arab Spring. Mohamed Bouazizi set himself on fire when police confiscated his vegetable and fruit cart because he lacked the proper permit. It was an act of despair and anger that resonated with predominantly young males in the Middle East who were deeply disappointed and disillusioned by their life situations, just barely scraping by despite what their governments had promised them. David recognized that the unequal distribution of wealth, widespread corruption, relative poverty, and decades of political repression had created a dangerous and highly combustible mixture in the Middle East. David and co-editor Mark Haas later published a highly regarded two-volume work on the Arab Spring in 2012 and 2017, analyzing the reasons behind game-changing events in the Middle East.

As the Arab Spring spread like wildfire across the region, Bashar thought that Syria was different and somehow immune from such domestic unrest, and at first the world seemed to agree. In early 2011 *Vogue* magazine sent one of its star authors, Joan Juliet Buck, to Syria to write a story, "The Rose of the Desert," about Asma al-Assad. The article featured vivid photographs of the country's ancient sites juxtaposed with images of its First Lady and president playing on the floor with their children. The family had grown since David had interviewed Asma. Hafez was now eleven, daughter Zein was nine, and the youngest son, Karim, was eight. Buck, like David, was touched by the glimpses of family life and the modernity of a mother who worked and lived in a relatively modest home, even if there were palaces within her reach.

Buck traveled to several cities with Asma to see projects that her NGO was supporting—a school, a health care complex, and an orphanage. She also gave her readers a peek at the First Lady's ongoing glamor, describing her fingernails, "lacquered a dark blue-green," and her Christian Louboutin red-soled shoes in vivid detail. The article presented a mostly positive portrait of a magnetic modern woman with big plans for a country she recognized was in the center of a "powder-keg region" of the world. The description proved horribly accurate. Shortly after the story ran, that powder keg exploded with violence and tragedy that revealed another picture of the Assads. *Vogue*'s publisher removed Buck's glowing article from the magazine's website and quietly tried to eradicate it elsewhere.

Early calls by anti-Assad elements for protests like those erupting in Tunisia, Egypt, Yemen, Bahrain, Libya, and nearby Jordan had failed to elicit much response in Syria. But during the first week of March 2011 at a school in Daraa, a city located near the Jordanian border, a group of teenaged students wrote

"Down with the Regime" on the wall of their school. Local security officials arrested them and sent them to Damascus for interrogation, while the regional governor, who was Bashar's cousin, did nothing. As frantic parents negotiated for their children's release, rumors swirled that the students had been tortured. On March 15 a few hundred protestors gathered at the mosque in Daraa. The crowd grew substantially in the following days and Syrian forces cracked down, killing at least fifteen civilians and wounding hundreds. Protests quickly spread to other cities, and well-informed Syria-watchers recognized that the country had become a pressure cooker about to explode.

On March 29 David wrote an opinion piece for the *New York Times*, "The Syrian President I Know." It concluded with the hope that "the unrest in Syria may have afforded President Assad one last chance at being someone more than simply Hafez al-Assad's son." As history documents, Bashar missed that chance, and in April David wrote another op-ed for the *Times* openly criticizing the Syrian president's handling of the uprising. Others followed in the *Financial Times*, the *Boston Globe*, *New York Daily News*, and the *Washington Post*. In the months that followed, he was no longer a welcome figure in Damascus. But he sent several notes via email to Bashar suggesting how the president might move through the crisis in a positive way that would not result in the dangerous collapse of his country. They were not answered directly, but two years later when David met in Damascus with Bouthaina Shaaban, a government minister and Bashar's political and media adviser, she told him that the president had read them carefully and that some of his ideas had been presented at cabinet meetings, but none were adopted. As protests increased and intensified, so did the government's response. And as the death toll rose, it was clear that blunt force had become the chosen deterrent to future demonstrations. In June 2011 Human

Rights Watch published a scathing fifty-five-page report on the Syrian crisis, "We've Never Seen Such Horror: Crimes against Humanity by Syrian Security Forces."

That same month journalist and political adviser Sidney Blumenthal brought David into a top-secret dialogue with Secretary of State Hillary Clinton. Blumenthal served as an aide and senior adviser to President Bill Clinton and remained a close confidante of Hillary Clinton when she became secretary of state for the Obama administration. Emails from her archive contain David's firsthand observations about the situation unfolding in Syria and extraordinary insights about that country's president. Eventually declassified in 2015, the emails read like a fast-paced thriller. They reveal insider information about Bashar al-Assad, his strengths and weaknesses, his difficulties with his security apparatus, the possibility of an International Criminal Court referral, and much more—all illustrating David's advisory role at the very highest levels of the US government. Blumenthal told Clinton that David was "perhaps the US expert with the closest relationship to Bashar al-Assad," and the information found in the archive, available on Wikileaks, demonstrates that Blumenthal was correct.

By 2012 an array of international humanitarian aid groups and conflict negotiation organizations had added Syria to their lists of countries in peril, and news stories coming from Western journalists still working in the country were alarming. A week after the UN's statement, a thirty-year-old American photojournalist, Austin Tice, was detained at a checkpoint near Damascus and presumably taken prisoner by Syrian security forces. A veteran captain in the US Marine Corps and graduate of Georgetown University, Tice had been working on a story about the ongoing conflict in Syria and its impact on the ordinary people that Bashar had so often told Asma he cared about. Tice had completed his final interviews

Photojournalist Austin Tice disappeared in Syria in 2012

and was headed to Lebanon for a thirty-first birthday celebration when he disappeared. Five weeks later a forty-three-second video was released to the media with the title "Austin Tice Is Alive." It showed the journalist being held by a group of armed men. His parents, Marc and Debra Tice, started an immediate campaign to engage government leaders, international agencies, the media, and the general public in working for his release.

The daughter of one of Debra Tice's dearest friends was attending Trinity University at the time and knew about David's biography of Bashar and his unique access to Syrian government officials. Debra did not hesitate to enlist David's help. "He listens in such a unique way," she says, "without preparing his response in advance. He really listens." Of course, David joined a diverse and expanding team of people to make inquiries at the highest levels of government, urging more careful listening, and hoping for answers and Austin's return.

As the situation in Syria escalated, the United States, Canada, Australia, Switzerland, and the European Union imposed new economic sanctions and restrictions on the country and called for Bashar al-Assad to step down from the presidency. The United States placed an embargo on the oil sector, freezing the financial assets of several individuals—including Bashar's cousin Rami Makhlouf; Ghazi Kanaan, the minister of interior affairs; and Rustum Ghazaleh, chief of military intelligence for Lebanon—and those of the Syrian state. Toward the end of 2011 the Arab League announced sanctions as well. Some diplomats with long years of experience in the Middle East still hoped the growing crisis could be turned around before total civil war broke out. Geir Pedersen, the Norwegian ambassador to the United Nations, who would later become the UN's special envoy to Syria, was one of those officials. He had been a member of the Norwegian team during the negotiations in Oslo that led to the Declaration of Principles in 1993 (the Oslo I Accord) and had served as the Norwegian representative to the Palestinian Authority before working for the United Nations in a variety of roles, including special coordinator for Lebanon. Pedersen knew the region well and was quick to see the value of a project that David and a coterie of impressive collaborators developed in late 2012.

Despite its rather cumbersome name, the Harvard-NUPI-Trinity Syria Research Project (HNT) was comprised of an extraordinary core team with a deep knowledge of both Syria and conflict resolution. Members included William Ury from the Harvard Negotiation Project; Frida Nome, Henrik Thune, and Mikkel Frøsig Pedersen from the Norwegian Institute of International Affairs (NUPI); George Saghir, a Syrian-American international financier with strong connections and family still in Syria; and David Lesch, the project lead. It expanded into an immense collaboration, enlisting the participation of more than a hundred people associated with diverse organizations and governments from around the world. The bulk of the project's funding came from the Norwegian Ministry of Foreign Affairs, thanks to Pedersen's strong support, and from Switzerland's Federal Department of Foreign Affairs due to another champion of the project, the Swiss Ambassador to the UN, Paul Seger.

Based on the concept that conflict can only be understood and analyzed when all viewpoints and perspectives are considered, the project's first mission was to "listen and learn." The leaders soon learned—as they had suspected—that there was not one overarching narrative describing the course of events of the Syrian uprising and conflict. They listened to each "side" that could be identified—Syrian government and pro-government officials, internal Syrian opposition leaders, and external officials who were either pro-opposition or neutral in their views. The conversations were complicated and ever-changing and had domestic, regional, and international dimensions. They interviewed hundreds of people over the next nine months and began to assemble those dimensions like pieces in a giant kaleidoscope, with a myriad of variations on the story with every turn. Their seventy-page executive summary, produced in late 2013, is filled with firsthand information obtained from people living throughout the political and human landscape. It contains none of the usual "bureaucrat speak" so often found in official reports, and its summary is chilling but not hopeless. It concludes with a "Common Ground Matrix" that identified areas of convergence and divergence, threads that offer a possible road to peace.

The same questions were asked at each face-to-face interview. Five focused on the present: the reasons for the conflict, whether the government could have prevented its escalation, whether it had lasted longer than expected, what obstacles were preventing resolution, and whether the UN had played a positive role. The first group to be interviewed was comprised of twenty leading figures from the Syrian opposition who were working in the country. That number more than doubled as the project progressed. No one associated with Jabhat al-Nusra (Al-Nusra Front) or any other groups labeled as jihadist was included. For security reasons, the meetings took place just across the Syrian border, in Gaziantep, Turkey, and were largely set up by Nir Rosen, a respected journalist and author who worked at the Centre for Humanitarian Dialogue in Geneva and was embedded with various Syrian opposition groups. The interviews were conducted by David, Ury, Saghir, Rosen, and David's research assistant, Jacob Uzman, a senior at Trinity University who was catapulted into an extraordinary drama that would cement his lifelong interest in the Middle East and its complexities.

With guidance from his professor and others on the team, Uzman participated in the ten- to twelve-hour days of interviews and was profoundly moved by what he heard. He remained in Turkey until the day before Christmas Eve 2013 and was not sure he would make it back to the United States. "We were supposed to fly out of Gaziantep to Istanbul to catch connecting flights home," he remembers, "but a thick fog rolled into the airport, preventing all planes from taking off."

> It was late in the evening, and it was unlikely that the fog would lift. Like other travelers, including a local soccer team, we were stranded. The agent told us there was a flight out of Adana in about two and one-half hours. It takes that long to drive to Adana in clear weather, but a local taxi driver told us he could make it in two hours. All five of us crammed into the taxi and set off through the fog to try to catch flights home to our families. As our taxi driver barreled through the dense fog along a winding Turkish highway, some feelings of trepidation crept in. It was extremely difficult

to see the road in front of us, but to make our flight we needed to travel at 100 or 120 kilometers an hour. At one point George [Saghir] half-jokingly told the taxi driver that making the flight didn't matter if we died along the way. Ultimately we made it to Adana, and as we were throwing our luggage through security, we saw the local soccer team that had been at the Gaziantep airport comfortably sitting at our gate, having braved the fog even faster than we did.

The adventure on that invisible road ended happily, with everyone safely home by Christmas. But the young researcher understood that it was not likely to be the case for the opposition fighters whom he had interviewed.

Almost everyone in the interview group felt that the Syrian government should have reacted decisively at the first signs of crisis instead of waffling about a response. There were strong feelings that Bashar should have fired his cousin, the governor of Daraa, immediately after the fiasco with the schoolchildren and that he should have gone there in person, possibly preventing the escalation of protests and violence that occurred. The Syrian opposition leaders who were interviewed overwhelmingly agreed that the conflict had lasted much longer than they had expected. Some stated that they would never have joined the revolution had they known it would be so lengthy and destructive.

When asked about the obstacles to resolving the conflict, answers were varied, but the most consistent one concerned the absence of international resolve, with particular blame on the United States for its lack of leadership after its call for Bashar to step down in late 2011. One secular revolutionary member added that "the Americans made a foolish move when they put Jabhat al-Nusra on the terrorism list. It's like they have a relationship with Bashar. They will only make Jabhat al-Nusra more strong with this." Several others lamented the fact that Syria did not have a nationalist leader who could unify the various internal groups, and all forty interviewees were unanimous in saying the United Nations had not played a positive role, and it was now too late.

One militia leader was a Sunni Muslim with a love for Italian opera and Spanish literature. The interview team invited him to dinner at the hotel in Gaziantep, and the meal was presented in several elaborate courses. According to David, the man had been going through so much deprivation and suffering that he could not eat. He did not feel it was right, knowing what his men were experiencing, but the "longing in his eyes" was forever etched in David's memory. Another militia leader was interviewed the day after his family had been killed by a barrel bomb in Aleppo. He was emotional and angry and said that the Americans weren't doing enough to help. An imam who had lived through the massacre at Hama ordered by Hafez al-Assad in 1982 described how half of the city had been leveled, and how he wanted revenge for that atrocity thirty years later. The imam asked David to pray with him privately after the meeting, and they did so in an adjoining room in the suite. Still another militia leader took off his shirt to show David and Ury terrible wounds from just a month of fighting, and one admitted that he had executed an enemy fighter earlier that day. The interviews were not easy. One of the top opposition leaders called David "the ambassador of the revolution," explaining that he and other opposition groups had been circulating his interview reports and talks criticizing the Assad government, and that those had an important galvanizing effect on the revolution.

The stories of torture and death and anguish were heartwrenching, and they had a profound effect on David. At one point, after a particularly emotional interview, he asked the militia leader why he was fighting against the regime and going through such an excruciating experience. The man replied, "Because I have heard my voice for the first time. Even in the mayhem and destruction, my voice is being heard by my people and they are beginning to make decisions on their own." David learned he was killed a few months later, but his words—and those of others brave enough to step forward—were part of a profound lesson in that small hotel on the Turkish border.

The other twelve interview questions focused on the future. Would the fighting still be underway in a year? Could the Syrian government suddenly collapse? Could a partition of Syria be possible, perhaps along sectarian lines? Was a phased transition a possibility? Would there be a deep purge if Bashar were to step down? Should the Ba'ath Party and the mukhabarat be eliminated? Were there concerns about growing Shiite influence and a stronger relationship with Iran? Should there be concern among minority groups about possible revenge killings? Could there be regional autonomy for Syrian Kurds? Would there be a new constitution? Would the new Syria be an Islamic state? And finally, what might be ahead for the 2014 Syrian election, when Bashar al-Assad was certain to run for another seven-year term? The answers were incredibly informative. Government agencies and the United Nations now had a detailed understanding of the tremendous obstacles to resolution of the Syrian conflict. The next steps would entail figuring out how to find the common ground essential to solutions. A large and dedicated team was ready to tackle the task, and David took the lead in compiling the results.

Wendy Pearlman, an author and a professor of political science at Northwestern University, was also listening to Syrian voices, chronicling hundreds of stories she collected between 2012 and 2017. In her 2017 book *We Crossed a Bridge and It Trembled: Voices from Syria*, she presents verbatim interviews that describe and reflect on life before, during, and since the start of the Syrian rebellion. The people she spoke to were victims of the conflict and part of the government opposition. She used pseudonyms to protect them from future retaliation. Some still lived in Syria, and others were in exile in Europe and elsewhere. Like David, she was profoundly moved by what she heard. A writer from Suwayda told Pearlman that she just whispered the word "freedom" during her first demonstration, until it became a shout. "When I heard my voice, I started shaking and crying. I felt like I was flying. I thought to myself, 'This is the first time I have ever heard my own voice.' I thought, 'This is the first time I have a soul and I am not afraid of death or being arrested or anything else.' I wanted to feel this freedom forever. And I told myself that I would never let anyone steal my voice again."

David continued to collect stories too. He traveled with the HNT group to Paris, London, Beirut, Amman, and Cairo to meet with Syrian opposition leaders in exile. In Paris he and Uzman interviewed a member of the second most powerful family in the country after the Assads, who was living incognito in a Left Bank apartment. Another exiled leader, Abdullah al-Dardari, had been Bashar's deputy prime minister and lead economic adviser before the civil war began and was then working for the World Bank in Geneva. The net was thrown still wider to include officials from foreign governments in Europe, Russia, and other countries in the Middle East. Each had his or her own lens to view the Syrian civil war. Judy sometimes traveled with David as he crisscrossed the world for meetings with government officials or presented findings from work in Syria to international organizations. From Moscow to Jerusalem, from London to Abu Dhabi, her presence softened the hard realities of what he had seen and heard about in Syria.

As always, David wanted to hear all sides of the evolving story,

Judy Dunlap and David Lesch, Muscat, Oman, circa 2013

and in February 2013 he arranged through Bouthaina Shaaban's government office to visit Damascus with Frida Nome as representatives of HNT. Martin Griffiths, a UN diplomat working on reconciliation agreements and ceasefires, accompanied them, and they met first in Beirut at the Phoenicia Hotel. After a dinner of long and serious conversation, and David's frequent expressions of empathy for the people caught in the crossfire of war, the diplomat smiled and said, "You are such a nice guy, but you

DEATH AND DIPLOMACY

don't have to be." The morning of the planned trip, Griffiths had received information that Damascus was surrounded by opposition militias but that the drive from the Lebanese border to the Syrian capital "should be pretty safe except for the random artillery fire and IEDs [improvised explosive devices]."

They made the unanimous decision to undertake the journey, and Bassam Hajjar, a Syrian businessman and friend of David's who was living at the Phoenicia Hotel, arranged for his car and driver to take the group to the border checkpoint. They were met there by Syrian government officials in two black sedans. Official visas were issued, and the cars raced down the highway to Damascus at top speed, the drivers hoping to reduce their vulnerability to shooting underway in the area. They passed burnt-out military vehicles, were waved through military checkpoints without stopping, and arrived in Damascus, where the constant rumble of artillery fire on Mount Qasioun echoed through the city. They met for two hours with Shaaban and Khaled al-Ahmad, a Syrian security head and trusted government emissary who would later be described in Western media as "a secret diplomat" and "mystery fixer." The HNT group shared insights for building bridges between the government and diverse opposition factions. Those recommendations proved crucial to Ahmad's negotiations of Bashar's reconciliation agreements in towns and villages across the country, effectively ending the violence of five years of civil war in 2017.

After the meeting the group went to lunch at a nearby restaurant, accompanied by both Syrian and UN security guards. During the meal Shabaan asked David, Nome, and Griffiths if they wanted to spend the evening in Damascus and leave the next morning. If not, she wanted the official drivers to make the round trip to the Lebanon border while it was still daylight. David looked at Griffiths for a signal, knowing the diplomat could

Syrian government officials (from left) Khaled al-Ahmad and Bouthaina Shaaban with Martin Griffiths, David Lesch, and Frida Nome, Damascus, Syria, 2013

assess the dangers involved with staying overnight. Griffiths gently shook his head no, indicating that it was best to return to Beirut, so David politely declined the offer. Once again the cars raced through the active war zone at a breakneck speed.

Other international organizations had also watched the Syrian civil war expand and focused new efforts on conflict resolution in the region. Conflict Dynamics International was such a group, and founder and CEO Gerry McHugh contacted David to explore ways to partner with the HNT project. McHugh was born in Ireland and had worked as a nurse in Baghdad during the Iraq war. That experience convinced him there had to be a better way to deal with conflict other than "patching people up after the fact." He had earned graduate degrees at the Massachusetts Institute of Technology and Cambridge, been a research fellow at the Center for International Conflict Studies, and worked with nongovernmental agencies including Save the Children UK and Concern Worldwide before cofounding Conflict Dynamics in 2004 with Allison Spaxman and Chris Saunders. The organization focused on the needs of children involved in armed conflict and on humanitarian aid and the de-escalation of violence in Sudan and Somalia. After the civil war began in Syria in 2011, McHugh became aware of the increasingly disturbing reports about the situation there and contacted David out of the blue.

"Let's talk," was David's immediate response. McHugh flew to San Antonio in September 2013 and immediately recognized a kindred spirit. There was instant rapport between the two men, but to McHugh's surprise David burst out laughing when he watched a presentation about Conflict Dynamics. What could possibly be funny about the serious work underway to alleviate suffering? The organization's logo contains a lion, and David quickly explained that in Arabic "Assad" means lion, and he wondered how the Syrian opposition would react to that symbol.

The partnership went forward despite the logo. McHugh brought many of the lessons learned in the Sudan during his organization's long years of work there, including a familiarity with the use of detainment, imprisonment, and hostage-taking by opposing factions that often are a terrible part of war. David continued to meet with the Tice family in Houston and US government officials, hoping he could help find some answers about their son's disappearance. According to the Syrian Network for Human Rights, disappearances and detainments had increased at an alarming rate along with reports of rampant torture in the detainment centers.

The first reports of chemical attacks also surfaced. In April 2013 the *New York Times* published a story about chemical weapons being used by the Syrian government in Aleppo, Homs, and possibly Damascus. The newspaper's source was a confidential letter from the British and French governments to the UN secretary-general. In August there was another attack and several mortars hit central Damascus near the Four Seasons Hotel. David recalled his first meeting with Hrair Balian in that elegant hotel in 2009, when there was still hope that Jimmy Carter and Bashar al-Assad would take a walk together along the proposed Abraham Path. Now, four years later, UN inspectors were staying there while they investigated the possibility of chemical warfare. Their visit became even more harrowing when they encountered sniper fire as they approached Ghouta, where another sarin gas attack was reported. They visited clinics, collected samples, interviewed survivors and doctors, and submitted their report to the UN. It was published in September 2013 and states that "the environmental, chemical, and medical samples we have collected provide clear and convincing evidence that the surface-to-surface rockets containing the nerve gas sarin were used in Ein Tarma, Al Moadameyah, and Zamalka in the Ghouta area of Damascus."

Despite the increasingly dangerous situation, Balian continued to travel in Syria's rural areas. He was documenting the destruction and abject poverty as people in the countryside grappled with the hard realities of drought, climate change, and civil war. The economic chasm was enormous between urban areas where a middle class had obtained most of life's necessities and rural areas where people had nothing, and it was tearing modern Syria apart. To make matters worse, neighboring Turkey, the source of all water coming into the country, was building new dams and holding back ever more water. A desperate situation was becoming worse.

David and Balian sometimes traveled into the Syrian countryside to listen to those living in the harshest circumstances. As before, Beirut was the starting point, and as they approached the

Syrian resistance fighters near Aleppo, 2013

Syrian border they were alarmed to see hundreds, if not thousands, of people at the checkpoint waiting to enter Lebanon. There was no line waiting to enter Syria, and they stepped right up to the checkpoint booth. The agent took one look at Balian's American passport and with a look of disgust threw it on the floor. He told him Americans weren't wanted in Syria. Balian politely picked up the passport and opened it to the page with a special visa granted by the country's foreign minister. The agent's face contorted with regret. After effusive apologies, the Americans were offered coffee followed by more apologies. Unpredictability was a part of every journey into a country where civil war was escalating. On another trip, after arriving in Aleppo on a flight from Jordan, Balian again presented his passport at the immigration booth. The agent jumped to his feet and saluted. Balian looked back to see if there was someone else standing behind him, perhaps a general, being saluted. With excitement, the officer said, "I've seen you on television with my president!"

Just two years after actor Angelina Jolie had visited Iraqi refugee camps on the Syrian border and dined with the Assads in Damascus, she visited camps in Turkey, Lebanon, and Jordan. This time the refugees were Syrian. Jolie, the UN's special envoy for refugees, was horrified to learn that nearly 1.7 million people had fled the brutal civil war, and that in 2013, Jordan's Zaatari refugee camp was housing more than 120,000 people, seven times the capacity it was built for. CNN reported that despite the ongoing war in Syria there had been little talk among world leaders about the humanitarian crisis. One reporter announced that "instead, the discussion at the recent G8 conference centered on whether the United States will arm the rebels fighting Bashar al-Assad's regime."

Lebanon's Hezbollah and the Iranian Revolutionary Guards had now openly deployed troops and advisers to prop up the Assad government, and by 2014 the rise of ISIS and other hardline Islamist groups had created the Islamic State caliphate. The prediction made by many of the opposition leaders during their interviews with David had come to pass. A different sort of war was energized, one that would prompt direct US military intervention and a whole new playing field.

Ambassador Jeffrey Feltman was serving as the under-secretary-general for political affairs at the United Nations, overseeing its peace and security work in many countries of the world, when he met David in 2014. He had spent decades in the Middle East as a former US ambassador to Lebanon, as assistant secretary of state for Near Eastern affairs, and in diplomatic posts in Erbil, Baghdad, Jerusalem, Tel Aviv, Tunis, and Amman. In his capacity at the UN, he was the chief policy adviser to the secretary-general, charged with helping the UN facilitate an end to the Syrian civil war. He recognized that the obstacles to peace were huge and that the conflict was worsening. Familiar with

David's work in Syria and the unique relationship he had built with Bashar, he invited David to join a small group of people with diverse views and experiences to brainstorm about what might be done to bring the war to an end.

Feltman appreciated David's unique "insider/outsider perspective" on the country and its political dynamics and valued his deep understanding of Bashar al-Assad's personality and leadership style. None of the representatives from the UN had ever been as close to the president as David, which made him a surrogate Damascus insider, but his career as an academic also set him apart from the government officials with whom he worked. In Feltman's words:

> He was not defending indefensible Syrian government positions but rather helping the UN's Syria envoys and me understand what the probable reactions would be from Assad to various diplomatic proposals. But his "outsider" status is also useful: he is not a product of the UN or US government service, where officials quickly absorb and internalize certain processes and guardrails that can subconsciously inhibit creativity. "Can't bother with that idea for the Russians (or Americans) might veto it" would be a typical reaction from a UN official. David has no such inhibitions, meaning his hypothetical sketchpad for potential ideas is constantly expanding.

Mona Yacoubian, a vice president at the United States Institute of Peace, wrote that "Syria's war has been the most complex conflict to emerge from the 2011 Arab uprisings. At least twice—in the spring of 2013 and in mid-2015—the Assad regime almost collapsed. Its comeback is attributable largely to outside players. The war has evolved through five phases that, along the way, have embroiled foreign figures and militias (often on different sides) from dozens of countries, regional governments, and global powers."

Those outside players were now deeply invested in the game. In 2015 Russia deployed some its most sophisticated weaponry and air-defense systems in support of the Syrian government, and the roles of Hezbollah and Iran deepened as well. David was reminded of the thoughtful observations his students had made when learning about the 1956 pact between Syria had Russia, when weapons had been the lure for a partnership that certainly had endured.

More than six thousand miles away from the escalating tensions in Syria, David felt growing apprehension about something closer to home and very personal. His mother's health had been deteriorating for several years. She had developed dementia in 2014 and was moved into the assisted-living wing at a senior-living facility in Bel Air. In 2016 David and Judy planned to visit her during the Christmas holidays, but in October Margaret Lesch was admitted to the hospital, slipped into a coma, and was put on a respirator. David had firm instructions from his mother not to put her on life support, and with a heavy heart he informed the doctor of her wishes. He asked the doctor to whisper in his mother's ear before taking her off of the respirator, to tell her how much her two sons loved her. The extended Lesch family traveled to Baltimore the next day, and sons David and Bob gave eulogies at her memorial. The loss was a hard blow to grandson Michael, who had a special relationship with his "Nana," and David and Bob were heartbroken, remembering a mother whose first concern had always been for her two boys.

The year 2016 was a grim one for Syria as well. According to the Syrian Center for Policy Research, by early 2016 the death toll from the civil war had risen to 470,000 and more than 117,000 people had disappeared or been detained. The UN Office for the Coordination of Humanitarian Affairs reported more than 6 million internally displaced people and 4.8 million seeking refuge

David Lesch in meetings at the United Nations, 2013

abroad. While that country's troubles had been in the news for five years, in 2017 another sarin gas attack that killed ninety people, including thirty children, elicited television images that horrified the world. A joint independent investigation by the United Nations and the Organization for the Prohibition of Chemical Weapons found the Syrian government responsible for the attack. The legendary red line had been crossed. Or had it?

By mid-2018 the Assad regime had retaken major cities, including Aleppo, recaptured suburbs surrounding Damascus for the first time since 2013, and turned its sights on Daraa, the birthplace of the uprising. It seized the city and most of southwest Syria by summer 2018. Bashar's reconciliation agreements have been called forced surrenders by some, but no one doubts that they de-escalated the violence that plagued the country for five years. In a *New York Times* opinion piece, "Assad Has Won Syria. But Syria Hardly Exists.," cowritten with his Harvard colleague James Gelvin, David lamented the dire postwar conditions and urged Bashar to "reshape his political system to fit a new reality."

Erupting in the heart of the Levant, Syria's war created a rippling impact throughout the Middle East and reverberated deep into Europe. It sparked the largest humanitarian crisis since the end of World War II and introduced frightening elements that might fuel future conflicts. The rise of a new generation of jihadists, battlefield tactics that violate modern norms of armed conflict (e.g., chemical warfare), emerging technologies like drones, encryption, and social media, massive civilian displacements, and humanitarian needs that overwhelm the international assistance infrastructure all contributed to the bleak outlook in Syria and other parts of the Middle East.

Syria's complex religious-political landscape was composed of diverse voices. Personal narratives coalesced into a collective story that continued to take shape. Journalist Austin Tice and several others were still missing, and neighboring countries in the Middle East and in Europe confronted increasing challenges as Syrian refugees sought asylum. People who remained in Syria faced famine and a growing humanitarian crisis. There were more innings ahead in the longer game, and an expanding group of Syrians and their international counterparts studied the playing field and considered next moves. David was not about to abandon the challenge. Ideas for innovative conflict resolution initiatives were brewing with William Ury, Gerry McHugh, and Hrair Balian. New efforts to resolve the Austin Tice situation were underway, and new conversations with both Syrian resistance leaders and government officials were on the calendar. David delivered frequent presentations at the US State Department, White House, Pentagon, and United Nations in addition to his ongoing work as a professor at Trinity. "David is indefatigable," Jeffrey Feltman says. "He never gives up, no matter how impossible the mission seems."

Israel Defense Forces soldiers inside the Gaza Strip, December 22, 2023

PIONEERING THE POSSIBLE

David continued to balance frequent international diplomatic trips with his university responsibilities. His interactions with Geir Pedersen, appointed special envoy for Syria at the United Nations in early 2019, and other leaders of international agencies focused on the worrisome escalation of economic, humanitarian, and political woes in Syria. In his numerous reports to the UN Security Council, Pedersen presented an increasingly stark picture of a country in deep trouble. But he always concluded by restating the UN's commitment to the Syrian people, reminding the council and the international media that "we can never give up." David shared that commitment.

On October 7, 2023, a terrorist attack on Israel by Hamas and several other Palestinian militant groups brought the world's attention to the Middle East once again. It was unexpected and vicious. Terrible atrocities were reported. Civilians were massacred in twenty-one communities and more than 250 people, including thirty children, were taken hostage by Hamas. David received a confidential call from Washington and joined a seasoned team of negotiators working on release of the hostages. A few weeks after the attack, two Americans and two elderly Israeli women were released, and an Israeli soldier was freed during ground operations in Gaza. Over the next eight months additional hostages were rescued by Israel Defense Forces, and a deal between Israel and Hamas secured the release of more hostages in exchange for the release of Palestinians being held in Israeli prisons. But the violence escalated. Israel launched massive attacks in Gaza, and strikes erupted from inside Lebanon and Syria on occupied Golan.

The world watched it all unfold, and protests over the war exploded in Europe, the United States, and other parts of the globe as horrific images flooded the media. Fears of a dangerous, expanded war in the Middle East worried longtime experts in the region and beyond. As Syria's special envoy, Geir Pedersen was aware of the impact of the larger war on an already vulnerable Syria. During a press conference with international media in June 2024, he noted that in addition to the worsening security situation, nine out of ten people in Syria were living in poverty—a staggering 90 percent—and 17 million needed humanitarian assistance. Even more troublesome, according to the Norwegian diplomat, was the fact that no progress had been made on the political front. "To address the security and economy, we need progress on the political front," he told the international press corps in summer 2024. "And we need a more comprehensive approach. I have challenged all the key actors—the government, the opposition, and the international community—to engage with me bilaterally."

With the presence of at least six foreign countries in Syria, including Russia and Iran by invitation, there have been many key actors and influences, and a strictly Syrian-driven process for creating a future for its population has been absent. The government controlled parts of the country, and other areas have been influenced by terrorist groups and by Turkish fighters on the border. Syrian Democratic Forces have been bolstered by support from the United States. It's evident why Geir Pedersen lamented the lack of a comprehensive approach to a nationwide ceasefire and urged the Security Council to work to develop one. And since the Syrian government believed it had won and could stay in power, why would it enter a process that might diminish its authority, if not its very existence?

Bilateral engagement has always been David's strong suit. Listening to and learning from all sides was essential in his work with Ury and McHugh during the Syrian civil war. After a meeting in 2014 with Donna Hicks, a psychologist and professor of international affairs at Harvard, the team added another ingredient to the ever-evolving recipe for peace. Hicks had been working in the field of conflict resolution for years—in Northern Ireland, Cuba, Palestine, Israel, Libya, Colombia, South Africa, and Sri Lanka—and had identified a "silent conversation" taking place in war-torn regions. "I thought about a second conversation as happening under the table," she explained in a *Leading Boldly into the Future* interview with journalist Anne Pratt. That second conversation concerned human dignity. The unspoken words were, "How dare you treat us this way? Can't you see we are human beings? Can't you see we are suffering, and you are doing nothing about it?"

David and William Ury were moved by her clear and thoughtful research about the importance of human dignity and impressed with how building it into negotiations had made a difference in outcomes in the peace process in Sri Lanka. David thought it could be powerful in Syria as well, as it was in complete alignment with HNT strategies, and told Pedersen it could be a new way forward, focusing on healing and the common need for dignity as a foundation for negotiation and ultimately political settlement.

The Dignity of Syria Initiative was introduced at the European Institute of Peace conference in Brussels in 2017. It garnered some support, but ultimately the various international governments did not choose to fund it. "Sometimes a great idea has to wait for the correct circumstances to be implemented, and that can take time," David told Pedersen when they met six years later in New York in late 2023. Ury understood the waiting game all too well, pointing to the stalled Abraham Path Initiative as an example of an idea simmering on a back burner until the time was right. "This is a hundred-year project," he said. "We're going to see a lot of setbacks; we may not live to see the fruition of it. But that's fine because it's an intergenerational project that will go on for hundreds, maybe thousands, of years longer."

From years spent in war zones in Latin America, Asia, Africa, and the Middle East, Ury has witnessed horrors and hopelessness. But his bestselling books still reflect an optimistic spirit. "After all these years people ask me if I'm an optimist or a pessimist," he says, and laughs. "I used to answer that I was an optimist, but right now I like the answer that I am a 'possibilist.' I believe in human possibility and potential." His 2024 book, *Possible: How We Survive (and Thrive) in an Age of Conflict*, explores the idea that success is not so much about the future as it is about the present. "Where can we move right now?" Ury asks. "Where is the creative possibility where everyone else sees impossibility? Where can you find those cracks, those openings? David can find those. We are both students of history and we face the realities, but we don't hesitate to be open to different directions, and that's why we are working together to this day. I've been using a phrase that came to me not long ago: 'The mission may be impossible, but the company's good.' David is the quintessential possibilist."

Jeffrey Feltman is less hopeful. "Unlike what I would imagine are David's views, I am fairly pessimistic when it comes to regional peace in the Middle East," he says. "The Arab states, frustrated by the futility of years of isolating Syria, reengaged with

David Lesch, Jeffrey Feltman, and Gerry McHugh, Washington, DC, July 2023

Bashar al-Assad in the hopes that engagement would produce more results than isolation. I agree that isolation policies have run their course at this point, but reengagement did not address the fundamental concerns that the Arab states (in general) have with Assad. The smuggling of Captagon [an illegal synthetic stimulant] from Syria to the Arab world has increased, not decreased, since engagement.... I do not think we collectively have the patience, political will, sustained attention, or the right mixture of incentives and disincentives ('carrots and sticks') to nudge Syria from a quasi-pariah/half-failed state into a productive player in the Middle East."

As Feltman predicted, David has taken the long view, and so have his longtime collaborators Ury and Hrair Balian. Balian's commitment to conflict resolution is not only professional but also personal. As a child growing up in Lebanon, as part of an Armenian family that had survived that country's genocide in 1920, he heard whispered conversations at the dinner table. His parents and grandparents quietly spoke words like "deportation" and "slaughter." He understands Donna Hicks's premise that there is a profound emotional side to conflict resolution, and that human dignity is an integral part of the puzzle. "The most important thing is humility and trying to put yourself in the shoes of someone on the other side," he states. "It is empathy and the ability to really listen...If you have only done negotiations in luxury hotel rooms or conference rooms, that's not enough. You have to be in the trenches. You have to experience the bombardment, feel it on your skin, see the blood, and hear the reverberation of bombs in your head to be able to understand what it is like to be in a conflict. David has done that."

In May 2024, with the world's eyes on the war in Gaza via internet streaming and television screens exploding with those images, Balian listed what would be long-lasting and terrible consequences:

> There are more than 600,000 kids who have not been to school since the October 7 attack by Hamas, famine is just around the corner, family members and other children they know are getting killed on a daily basis. They are traumatized, and they will remain traumatized for the rest of their lives, I'm afraid. Also significant: they are ready fodder for extremist recruitment. They are the next

soldiers for whichever extremist organization offers them a few pennies and a few cigarettes. And of course, from a belief point of view, an ideological point of view, they will want to avenge what has happened to them. So we're in this conflict for a very long time. And this is not just about Gaza. We're talking about the West Bank. We're talking about Syria. We're talking about Lebanon. We're talking about the entire Middle East.

Balian has felt depressed and exhausted at times, especially when looking into the eyes of children in the crossfire. But like David and other "possibilists" in this ongoing drama, he treasures the small successes and is not about to give up. He explains quite simply, "We have no right not to try," an echo of Geir Pedersen's words to the international press.

Despite establishing good relations with both the government side and the rebel groups, and all the work done by David and so many others, the UN's efforts to incorporate and promote strategies for peace did not work. Balian blames both Bashar al-Assad and the West for the lack of success. "Assad was an unbelievably stubborn leader," he says, "and he would not give in even one iota regardless of what the benefits could be. He didn't trust anyone. I don't blame him for not trusting the West, but one still needs an element of trust in leadership. The West also has a huge responsibility in the failure because of its blind alliance with some of the opposition leaders who, if they came to power, would be as bad as Assad himself."

Ahmad Zahra has a different take on post–civil war Syria. He was born in Damascus but spent his early childhood in England, where his father studied and practiced medicine after serving as a general in the Syrian army. Zahra did not speak Arabic until he was ten years old, after the family moved back to Damascus and his father became the first neurosurgeon to practice in Syria.

The move itself was an adventure. The family drove from England to Syria, a long journey across more than ten countries, because Zahra's father knew it would be difficult to buy a new car in Damascus. When they reached Turkey, they had trouble finding a hotel. A couple that did not speak English or Arabic invited the Zahra family to stay in their large home. It was Ahmad's first experience with the hospitality and food of the Middle East, and he marveled as Turkish, Arabic, and English words swirled around a table loaded with exotic delicacies. After the family's arrival in Damascus, his grandmothers—who spoke no English—contributed to the speed with which he learned Arabic. He made friends and did well in school, earning a medical degree and becoming a physician like his father.

During a one-year internship in London in the late 1990s, Zahra had a chance meeting with another young physician named Bashar al-Assad. When Bashar's younger brother, Majd, developed neurological problems, the Assad family traveled to England to see a specialist there. Ahmad was doing an internship with the specialist, and because he was Syrian, he was invited to a luncheon during the Assad family's visit. He met Bashar, who appeared to be a shy introvert, similarly interested in medicine and music. "I never would have predicted that the young doctor sitting next to me was going to become the person he became."

Zahra returned to Damascus and practiced medicine for three years, specializing in pathology and fulfilling his father's hopes for him but not-so-secretly dreaming of a much different career. He loved movies and the worlds of art and cinema, but Syria was not the place for him to pursue such things. Being gay added another dimension to the struggle, and he knew that to truly find himself he needed to leave his country of origin. His father eventually gave his blessing to the idea. Zahra applied for visas, targeting England, Australia, Canada, and the United States. As he describes it, in 1996 he "won the golden ticket to America," one of only two people in a room packed with hopeful candidates who "hit the jackpot." Like Bashar, Zahra abandoned medicine, but unlike the Syrian president, his new calling was filmmaking not politics. He established Zahra Pictures in 2004 and began producing feature films and inspirational documentaries about community building. Ironically, a few years later, he added politics to his resume, becoming the first openly gay Arab immigrant to be elected city councilman in Orange County, California, and the first openly gay Muslim elected in the United States—a proud American devoted to the democratic process.

He and David met in 2008, three years before the Arab Spring, when hopes for the cultural walking trail project were still high and historic sites were being scouted for the route. Zahra was planning to produce a feature about Syria and was creating a photographic archive of those sites. He and David cowrote a screenplay, "The Reformer," about David's relationship with Bashar when there were still indications that the Syrian president might usher in a new style of leadership in Syria. The civil war effectively nixed that idea.

Zahra describes David as "a man who fell in love with the Middle East and its history, culture, and people, a man who wants to play a positive role there, a modern-day Lawrence of Arabia in a sense." While recognizing that British explorer/diplomat T. E. Lawrence has been criticized by some twenty-first-century historians for his naivete, Zahra believes that naivete also can be a harbinger of hope. And he sees hope in postwar Syria. "In the summer of 2023, I went back to Syria after thirteen years of absence because of the war," he says, "and I was so happy to see my family again." His eighty-three-year-old father still practices medicine in Damascus, treating at least half of his patients free of charge because they cannot pay. "I spoke to a young boy,

Al-Hamidiyah, souk in Damascus, 2023

perhaps eleven or twelve years old, who sells bread by the souk. His memories of the civil war are vague, only what his parents have told him, and he is hopeful about his future. I think most people in Syria are living life today with the reassuring knowledge that there *is* a tomorrow. During the war they weren't sure that was the case."

Because most of his old friends had left Syria, during his visit Zahra chatted with random people who shared their thoughts on the country's future. He enjoyed taking taxis all over the city, exploring Damascus and listening to diverse views. "Everyone said they prized security and safety. They were tired of conflict. There were a few who were courageous enough to share some political opinions, but not many. They were mostly critical of the interference by outside powers, whether East or West. For me, I was just happy to return to my birth country, see my family, enjoy the culture and the delicious food, and reminisce about my early life there."

Of course, outside powers have always paid close attention to Syria and the entire region. "There is no question that the Middle East is a mess," F. Gregory Gause III wrote in the March/April 2022 issue of *Foreign Affairs*. He and David Lesch first met when they were earning their doctoral degrees at Harvard in the late 1980s and cemented their bond on the basketball courts playing for the Center for Middle Eastern Studies Shaykhs. They have devoted nearly forty years to working on Middle East issues in wide-ranging capacities. Gause's long career in teaching, writing, and diplomacy has included professorships at Columbia and Harvard, fellowships at the Council on Foreign Relations and at the King Faisal Center for Research and Islamic Studies in Riyadh, Saudia Arabia, and the chairmanship of The Bush School of Government and Public Service at Texas A&M University. His *Foreign Affairs* article, "The Price of Order: Settling for Less in the Middle East," presents a thoughtful and thorough look at a complex history and confirms what Zahra discovered through his informal conversations with taxi drivers in Damascus: stability and order may be the best goals to strive for, for both obvious and more complicated reasons.

"It is in Syria, where the tension between order and liberal principles will play out most clearly," Gause writes. "An orderly Syria, able to prevent terrorist organizations from using its territory and, over time, put some distance between itself and its current Iranian and Russian patrons, would be better than the Syria that exists now.... As loathsome as Assad was, it would have made sense to recognize this reality and begin a process of contact with his government, at first to minimize the risks to the few American forces still in Syria but eventually to pursue the common interest of preventing Salafi jihadists from maintaining their foothold in the country." He says David is uniquely positioned to play an important role in reconnecting an orderly Syria, should the country achieve stability, to the United States in the years ahead.

Although David had not spoken directly to Bashar since 2009, channels of communication were not completely closed as recently as 2024. Kamal Alam, a senior fellow at the Atlantic Council, believed that opening those channels was essential to peace and prosperity in the Middle East. Originally from Pakistan, Alam is a former fellow at the Royal United Services Institute, the world's oldest defense and security think tank, and has admired David's research and writing since his university days. David's books were required reading for Alam's undergraduate courses at Durham University in England and provided a foundation when he earned his graduate degree in Syrian history at the University of Damascus. Alam's family connections to Syria run deep. Both of his grandfathers served in the Pakistan Air Force and worked closely with the Syrian military, and one was stationed in Damascus during World War II, where he met his future wife. When Andrew Bowen, a foreign affairs analyst who has worked for the American Enterprise Institute and other think tanks, introduced him to David, Alam was thrilled to meet the author of so many of the books he had studied and a man whose belief in building channels of communication had inspired him.

Today Alam specializes in Syrian relations and considers the

Syrian civil war to be "one of the most fateful wars of our time, a turning point that destabilized the whole region." He praises David's openness to dialogue with the Syrian government and calls it essential. He is of the opinion that the United States made a mistake in opposing Assad during the civil war and describes some of the opposition groups it supported as "mostly terrorists." While working at the Royal United Services Institute in 2017, Alam escorted a group of British generals to Syria for a firsthand look at what was going on. They traveled there with viewpoints held by most Westerners and discovered the complexities of the region and its factions, returning to England with a new perspective. This transformation was described in "The Road to Damascus: The Arabs March Back to Befriend Assad," an article that Alam and David coauthored for *War on the Rocks* in 2018. "David always has understood the need for firsthand information, obtained through careful listening. He was on the ground in Syria, really listening to all the nuanced stories, observing the authentic picture through multiple lenses," Alam says, "and realizing that democracy cannot be forced at the barrel of a gun."

Kevin Stryker, an attorney in Houston, took all of David's history courses at Trinity and traveled with him to Syria in 1995 as part of the Summer in Syria program. "I remember the first time I got into a taxi with him, he began asking the driver about himself and his family. I thought he was just being courteous until it happened over and over with drivers, shopkeepers, waiters. He wasn't just about connecting with the powerful and influential. He genuinely cared, learned from, and engaged with everyday people, not just with passing niceties but with real conversation."

Careful listening to nuanced stories and profound conversations have been an important part of Debra and Marc Tice's relentless search for information about their missing son, journalist Austin Tice. Their mission touches the heart of every

David Lesch with Debra and Marc Tice in Houston, Texas, 2020

parent, and the emotional toll of more than a decade of uncertainty about their son is unimaginable. In 2012, the same year that Austin disappeared in Syria, David and Judy discovered that Michael was bipolar, and it too seemed unimaginable. They were devastated by the knowledge that a young man who had once enjoyed a normal family life and shared wonderful adventures with them was suffering such mental anguish. In his early 20s Michael would vanish from home, traveling to other cities, and David would retrieve him for proper care in San Antonio while balancing more than 300,000 miles of global traveling for HNT and other diplomatic initiatives. As always, David listened and learned, attempted to understand the challenges at hand, tried to map a viable plan for Michael's treatment, and did not give up hope for a productive life for his son.

Likewise imbued with courage, perseverance, and hope, the Tice family's efforts to find Austin have garnered international support at the highest levels of government. David describes

Debra as a "force of nature," noting she can call the secretary of defense, the national security advisor, and the special envoy for hostage affairs on her telephone at a moment's notice. President Biden mentioned the Austin Tice case during the White House Correspondents' Dinner in 2024, calling on Syria to release the missing journalist, just as he had done in previous years. According to US intelligence sources, Austin is still alive. But the Syrian government has maintained that they do not know where he is, and this may be true.

David believes it is also possible that he is being held by a one-off militia group tied to the government, which provided Bashar Assad with plausible deniability and served as a bargaining chip for some future grand return. For a time, tidbits of information circulated that Austin had been taken to a hospital in Beirut. Questions linger about where he might be held if he is alive. In 2022 Erik Sunde, an international sanctions lawyer and good friend of the Tice family, joined the team working on the case. David introduced him to Bashar's father-in-law, Fawaz Akhras, who was a practicing cardiologist in London and someone David regularly visits when he is in the UK. Every path is worth exploring, and David meets often with Sunde and the Tice family, and with the Hostage Recovery Fusion Cell at Federal Bureau of Investigation (FBI) headquarters whenever he is in Washington.

David describes it as a "story with lots of ebbs and flows, where you think you are close and then something falls apart," and it touches him deeply. In 2019 he worked with several prominent Syrians who had direct access to the top decision makers in Damascus. There appeared to be an opportunity to find Austin Tice or at least gain credible information on him. In August David received a call from his government liaison within the National Security Council letting him know his Tice initiative had been approved and signed by national security advisor John

Bolton. Only five people knew about this top-secret plan and David's intention to travel to Damascus. He was encouraged that his diplomatic work had received "activation status," but the next morning he learned that Bolton had been fired (or had resigned, depending on which story one believes). Bolton's departure had nothing to do with the Tice initiative, but it effectively killed it. Appointment of his successor was delayed, and the new adviser did not activate it. It was an excruciating disappointment, but David still sought new paths forward.

A little later that year he attended a three-day conference in Washington sponsored by Cure Violence, an organization founded by epidemiologist Gary Slutkin. Slutkin had creatively applied the principles of containing epidemics to containing and reducing violent crime in cities across the United States, Latin America, and the Middle East. David admired the concept and was proud to serve on Cure Violence's board of advisors. The workshop was focused on how violence might be reduced in certain parts of Syria, and one session dealt with how to communicate that organization's important findings to President Donald Trump. After some discussion of conventional approaches, one participant, a former diplomat, noted that the best way to communicate with Trump was through the media, specifically through Tucker Carlson on Fox News, which Trump was known to watch. A plan took shape in David's mind. Perhaps if Debra Tice could appear on the show and appeal to Trump, he might make Austin Tice's release a priority, recognizing the tremendous positive publicity and goodwill that would create. David suggested the idea to Debra and Marc but admitted that he did not know Carlson. With her usual energy, Debra used her honorary membership in the foreign press to get in touch with the show producers. She appeared on February 28, 2020, and told viewers an incredible story. She said the US State Department had betrayed Trump, noting that the president had sent her a note in 2019 promising to do what he could. Trump saw the interview, and according to many insiders in his administration, was furious at the State Department.

The president wrote a personal letter to Bashar al-Assad with David's assistance, asking for the Syrian government's help to find the missing journalist. At David's insistence, Trump did not accuse the Syrians of taking him captive, and he simply asked for their help. David strongly suggested giving the letter to a prominent Syrian expat who could deliver it personally to Bashar in Damascus, but the Trump administration insisted on going through official channels. That meant going through the Czech embassy in Damascus, which represented American interests in Syria since the United States had closed its embassy early in the civil war. The Czech embassy would be responsible for delivering it to the Ministry of Foreign Affairs. As David feared, the letter most certainly was deposited in the black hole of the foreign ministry, where many eyes would read it, including members of the Syrian intelligence. He predicted that it might reach Bashar in an altered state or not at all. It was another missed chance resulting in deep disappointment for Debra and Marc, who continued to experience a rollercoaster of emotions. "I feel tremendous empathy for them," he says, "and we will not give up on this."

At the White House Correspondents' Dinner in 2022, keynote speakers brought up the disappearance of Austin and other journalists who had been detained or imprisoned in foreign countries and urged the While House to strengthen efforts to bring them home. The following Monday the Tices met with President Biden and a roomful of National Security Council advisers. Biden listened to Debra and Marc with compassion then walked to his desk and telephoned James Baker, former US secretary of state. Baker, then ninety-two years old, had maintained close relationships spanning decades with government officials around the world, especially in the Middle East, and Biden asked for his help. He also instructed his advisers in the room to pursue four goals in Syria. According to Debra, he told them, "Get in there. Listen to them. Find out what they want. Work with them to get Austin Tice home."

"Presidents seem to think that if they give instructions, they are followed," Debra said in 2024. "But it doesn't work that way. US officials did not engage with Syrian officials. We think our government works the way we were taught in seventh-grade civics class: it doesn't." But some of Baker's international colleagues did launch inquiries about Austin in 2022, including Lebanon's chief of intelligence, Major General Abbas Ibrahim. Debra constantly pursues her own international connections as well. She introduced David to Yousef Al Otaiba, the United Arab Emirates ambassador to the United States, who actively serves as a bridge between governments in the Middle East and has tried to discover information about Austin's situation.

Otaiba's father served as the UAE's first minister of petroleum and was president of OPEC six times, and he has put his power and influence behind his son's efforts to create positive change in the region. Educated at Georgetown University, Otaiba became senior adviser to Shaykh Mohamed bin Zayed Al Nahyan, the ruler of Abu Dhabi (and now president of the UAE), at age twenty-six and held several other high-level government positions in the UAE before becoming ambassador to the United States in 2008. He helped broker the Abraham Accords in 2020 and pushed hard for the Israel–United Arab Emirates peace agreement in 2022, marking the first time an Arab nation had normalized ties with Israel since Jordan in 1994. The ambassador called it "a win for diplomacy for the region," and the international community hoped it might encourage other nations to follow suit.

Otaiba's negotiating skills are undeniable and far-reaching. In addition to his assistance in the ongoing Tice investigation, he became enthusiastic about the Abraham Path Initiative when he learned it was considering expanding to other Middle East countries. In 2023 he and David brainstormed about how that might happen, with sites in the UAE becoming part of the historic trail, which would help attract partner countries in the Middle East. But after the Hamas attack in Israel and the resulting war in Gaza erupted, this idea for a path of peace in the UAE was put on hold—yet another case of events outside of one's control delaying progress on important initiatives.

According to Debra, the United States had spent more than $2 billion on the Hamas situation by mid-2024 and was negotiating hard for the release of the hostages in Gaza. "I told our national security advisor, Jake Sullivan, that surely someone who is already in the region could work on Austin's case at the same time," she says, remembering the message from Syrian officials in 2014 that they would only talk to a senior US government figure and not Austin's mother. It is possible she is correct when she suggests that "the Syrians want to engage." According to news agency Agence France-Presse, around the same time Bashar gave an enigmatic response to questions about communications with the West. Quoted as part of an interview with a Russian-backed official from Georgia's breakaway region of Abkhazia, published by Syria's official Sana news agency, the Syrian president said, "America is currently illegally occupying part of our lands... but we meet with them from time to time, although these meetings do not lead to anything."

Two other countries occupy part of Syria's lands by invitation: Russia and Iran. At the same time, F. Gregory Gause III believed that Iran was "the big winner in the Middle East's crisis today," noting that its outpouring of money, weapons, political and logistical support, and even fighters had solidified its influence in Syria and other vulnerable Arab states. David knew then that Iran was the most influential outside country in Syria in terms of military, political, economic, and cultural impact, although Russia also played an important role as a military ally. Both have had a long-term relationship with Syria, but David notes that both were in some competition with each other as well, vying for influence in the Syrian military and intelligence apparatus and for business contracts. "Bashar's father first established a relationship with Tehran in 1979, following the Egypt-Israel peace treaty," he says. "He was desperate for some strategic depth against Israel when Egypt signed on the dotted line. Syria supported non-Arab Iran against Arab Iraq in the Iran-Iraq War in the 1980s. Hafez al-Assad was more pragmatic than an idealogue. It has been the most important alliance Syria has maintained."

As Syria's civil war came to an end in 2017, David wrote about that alliance the *New York Times* opinion piece "Iran Is Taking Over Syria. Can Anyone Stop It?" He noted that "Iran came to Mr. Assad's aid to ensure its access to Lebanon and to keep Saudi Arabia from extending its influence in the Levant. The war looks set to end, eventually, with Mr. Assad still in charge, and in great debt to the country that enabled it to survive." David believed from his conversations with Bashar before the civil war that the Syrian president would have been willing to jettison or seriously downgrade his country's relationship with Iran and Hezbollah if he could have gotten a peace deal with Israel that would have returned the Golan Heights.

> There were some serious negotiations along those lines during Bashar's first decade as president, but when the Arab Spring and civil war occurred, Damascus was compelled to turn closer to Iran and Hezbollah, and now their footprints are deeper than ever in

David Lesch conducting an interview with ABC News, August 2013

Syria. In the last couple of years, however, some Arab Gulf states—primarily Saudi Arabia and UAE—have restored relations with Damascus and allowed Syria to return to the Arab League, in order to counter Iranian influence and to exert their own influence on Damascus because it sits in such a strategically important position.

David's understanding of intricate geopolitical issues remains much in demand by media outlets seeking to clarify Middle East events for their audiences. He has appeared frequently on CNN,

David Lesch and Judy Dunlap at Yankee Stadium

Fox News, Al Jazeera, the BBC, NPR, and many other platforms. He has been interviewed by Anderson Cooper, Wolf Blitzer, Brooke Baldwin, Shepard Smith, and countless other journalists. Judy has observed a special talent, whether on a television news show, participating in a roundtable of experts, or enjoying a dinner with good friends, that elevates her husband to a possibilist, William Ury's term. "People quickly turn to him for thoughtful leadership," she says. "He has an innate ability to get straight to the point without ever trying to dominate the conversation. Before you know it, he is summing up what he has heard in a way that makes everyone feel included and important." His former student and friend Tom Ewald first noticed this talent during David's television broadcasts following the Iraqi hostage situation in 1990. His public charisma was undeniable.

Pulitzer Prize–winning author Doris Kearns Goodwin has said

that the most underappreciated aspect of leadership is the ability to find time to relax and replenish one's energies. In a 2020 interview with Karen Given on Boston's WBUR, she mentioned that regular nights at the theater provided recovery time for Abraham Lincoln. Franklin Roosevelt delighted in evening cocktail parties where no talk of politics was allowed. David Lesch has naturally sought needed relaxation and relief from his grueling travels in attending baseball games with Judy, even when they root for opposing teams, as when the New York Yankees battle the Baltimore Orioles. Like David, baseball is one of Goodwin's special joys, something she considers much larger than a game. She credits it with making her a better historian, a reminder that "we just don't know how it's going to end" and must therefore watch it unfold from beginning to end.

Baseball has been a steadfast source of both inspiration and connection in David's life as well. Early in his teaching career at Trinity, he made a friend who might have been his boss back in his pitching days. When they met in the 1990s, Tom Kayser was president of the Class AA Texas League, a position he held for twenty-five years. Formed in 1902, more than ninety-one minor league teams in Texas, Arkansas, Kansas, Louisiana, Missouri, and Oklahoma were associated with the league over its long history. Prior to assuming the presidency, Kayser enjoyed various roles in the sport he loved, including as scout for the Pittsburgh Pirates and the Cincinnati Reds and as owner of a Milwaukee Brewers minor league club. When the two men met through a mutual friend and professor at Trinity, they felt an immediate rapport. "It was as if I had known David all my life," Kayser says. David recounted the story about attending Central Arizona College, training in the Mars-like desert of Arizona, and how his coach had kept him hidden from the major league scouts, saving him for the Milwaukee Brewers. Had the Dodgers not staged their clever ruse to recruit him first as their number one draft pick, David probably would have played for Kayser's double-A minor league team in the Brewers organization. The men also talked about how David eventually left the pitcher's mound for an entirely different game.

"In his conflict resolution work, David's doing today what he would have been doing on the mound," Kayser said, "figuring out how to get people to agree without endangering the position that he's holding." The lessons learned on the baseball diamond—work ethic, attitude, dealing with adversity, and overcoming obstacles—translated well to David's world of international diplomacy and business, and his students have grasped the authenticity of their multifaceted professor. An amateur historian and coauthor, with David King, of *Baseball in the Lone Star State: The Texas League's Greatest Hits*, Kayser shared his knowledge and firsthand experiences as a visiting lecturer for one of David's most popular courses, covering the history of baseball, taught during summer semesters at the University of Texas at Austin. Judy remembers that class well. She sat in on a few of David's lectures, prepared to see coeds swooning over her husband. "I was totally surprised by his classroom persona," she says, and laughs. "He was unapproachable on that personal level but managed to enthrall the class with his knowledge, always totally professional. I've seen his totally open side, of course, but I love the fact that his boundaries are clear and strong. That serves him well in his international work too. He creates a very safe space, and that is a real gift—for both a wife and the world."

Kayser says David is not "monofocused," and Kevin Stryker agrees. Kayser witnessed his courses bring baseball and its place in American society to life, and Stryker experienced the same depth and energy in his history of the Middle East classes. "He does not just describe what happened—the dates, the rulers, the battles aren't the point of his lectures," says Stryker. "He delves into the why and occasionally the what if of the history of the Middle East."

David's involvement in fascinating and diverse international projects adds still another dimension to his life. He worked with Hye Hong, head of business development at Philadelphia-based Ghost Robotics, to explore possible uses for the company's ground drones and four-legged-robots in the UAE. The remarkable machines look like something straight out of *Star Wars* and have numerous military and commercial applications. The US Army is experimenting with them, and Japan deployed them in its earthquake relief efforts in 2024.

David and Hong traveled to Abu Dhabi to showcase the company's Quadrupedal Unmanned Ground Vehicles (Q-UGVs)—four-legged robots that look like something from a galaxy far, far away—for the country's top technology conglomerate, G42. A contract was offered, but Ghost Robotics did not sign it for fear that G42 had been infiltrated by the Chinese, and the Pentagon did not want to see the technology in the hands of China. David has also collaborated with South Korean entrepreneur Yonghun Kim on a variety of endeavors in Guatemala, the Middle East, and Asia. Through his contacts at the National Security Council, he arranged meetings with President Biden for Kim and other South Korean business leaders, including the CEO of battery maker LG Energy Solution and the chair of the manufacturing conglomerate SK Group.

A touch of baseball and history also found its way into the international mix. César H. Cantú García is the CEO of the Alianza Group, a large holding company based in Saltillo, Mexico, involved in agricultural business, construction, and financial solutions. He also owns the Mexican Baseball League team Saraperos de Saltillo. Cantú approached David with several business

David Lesch shaking hands with Mexican politician Manolo Jiménez Salinas, now governor of Coahuila, Mexico, and Alianza CEO César Cantú García

ideas, including bringing a Mexican League team to San Antonio and creating a traveling exhibit for a natural history museum in Saltillo that would tour the United States and build a stronger bond with Mexico. Together they arranged for the Saraperos to visit for a series of exhibition games.

San Antonio remains David's home base, both literally and figuratively. He and Ron Nirenberg, who served as mayor from 2017 to 2025, were introduced by Bill Clover in late 2016 and have worked together on diverse local, national, and international projects. Although he was at Trinity soon after David began teaching there, Nirenberg did not take any of his classes and David jokingly reminds the mayor of this. Nirenberg has seen David earn accolades and awards from the university for scholarship, research, and teaching, and he believes his colleague and friend is doing some of his most important work on that campus: preparing the next generation of leaders.

Jackie Montaine, now a consultant in Washington, DC, agrees. She graduated from Trinity in 2011 and credits the education she received there with preparing her for "a world in which technology, geopolitics, and even the way society connects are shifting in real time. Dr. Lesch was a huge part of why that education was so valuable. The skill level, intelligence, and global aperture he has brought to that academic institution has raised the game for all of us." She remembers a few classes being cancelled when David was called to Washington to testify about Syria in front of the US Senate and the excitement she felt knowing she had the opportunity to learn the same information that policymakers were using. Many of David's students pursued careers in national security and international relations, and all describe their former professor's high expectations with gratitude. "We were encouraged to work hard and perform well," Montaine says. "When I learned more about Dr. Lesch's background, including his baseball career, it made me appreciate that performing well was a matter of choice in life, and that the output of those decisions showed up in multiple aspects of life."

Carey Latimore was an outstanding scholar of Black history and the codirector of Trinity University's African American studies minor. He considered David an important mentor during his early years at the university and eventually succeeded him as chair of the history department in 2011. Latimore credited David with building a new culture within a department that had known its share of dysfunction in the past, one that turned its focus to "inclusive excellence." The two professors became great friends, and David served as best man when Latimore married his wife, Almie. He was devastated when Latimore was diagnosed with

David Lesch being honored for thirty years of service at Trinity University, with university president Vanessa Beasley, 2023

cancer in 2020 and died at age forty-six. "He put other people at ease when talking about difficult subjects," David wrote in a *San Antonio Express-News* article after Latimore's death. "He always listened and was always willing to hear different perspectives. He had a very distinct method of leadership that really worked, and it was a combination of patience, understanding, empathy, and compassion."

Trinity University president Vanessa Beasley recognizes the

importance of a stellar faculty and notes that it is a big reason the school is ranked as one of the country's best liberal-arts universities. "David Lesch is one of Trinity's most sought-after professors," she says. "His scholarship on a variety of topics, most of which concern the Middle East, has positioned him as a global thought leader, advising multiple presidential administrations, the United Nations, and high-level officials across the globe. Yet no matter where his expertise and experiences take him, Professor Lesch always brings it all back to Trinity students, literally helping prepare our students for both the realities and the nuances of an increasingly complex world."

Kevin Stryker adds that, besides being a talented teacher, mentor, historian, and policy advisor, his former professor embodies empathy. "Far more important to those around him, he's a good man. A good father. A good husband. A good friend." It's a strong combination of roles that is—or should be—a model for human behavior. David chooses the proverbial high road in meeting the challenges and opportunities in the modern Middle East, where oil, religion, conflict, and history are no longer the only bridges between the region and the West. Compassion and understanding for others, as he has amply demonstrated, inspire people who are eager and willing to tackle problems—local or global—on a human level: true "pioneers of the possible."

Fall of the Assad regime, Damascus, December 2024

SYRIAN SURPRISE

On Saturday, December 7, 2024, the world was jolted by new and unexpected events unfolding in Syria. For the past few years international news outlets had reported on a growing but fragile stability in the country. Several Arab countries had reintegrated Assad's government into their diplomatic circle, and Western powers were adjusting to the inevitability that Syria's leader was there to stay. In 2019 David had expressed his interest in meeting Bashar again, to see how their worldviews had matured over the last decade and to share the diverse ideas he had gathered during his interviews with Syrian opposition groups. He was hopeful about finding common ground that might lead to positive changes in a nation that was struggling economically, politically, and emotionally.

But in the late hours on that Saturday, and into early Sunday morning, a surprise startled the world. Syrian rebels executed a powerful push into the strategic hubs of Aleppo and Homs and were closing in on Damascus. Led by the Sunni Islamist group Hay'at Tahrir al-Sham (HTS), rebels advanced quickly against Syrian government forces, and their success startled even themselves. HTS leader Abu Mohammad al-Jolani urged the Syrian military to lay down their arms, promising that soldiers would not be harmed. The soldiers did just that, many leaving their uniforms behind.

By Sunday morning Syria's longtime ally, Russia, urged its citizens to leave the country, and Iran continued a withdrawal of its military commanders that had started quietly a few days before. The world wondered if the powerful Assad dynasty, led first by Hafez and then by his son Bashar—presidents for an era spanning more than fifty years—was going to topple as the end of 2024 approached. Expectations among government supporters were that Bashar would address the nation, but he did not. The state media denied rumors that he had fled to Moscow, Tehran, or the United Arab Emirates. Staff in the presidential palace had assisted a film crew set up for a television address by Assad to reassure the nation and announce a plan to share power with members of his political opposition. But Assad was nowhere to be found. Even his closest aides wondered where he was.

Meanwhile rebels had won back territory in the north. Other opposition groups in the south seized Daraa, considered by some to be the birthplace of the Syrian civil war in 2011. As Sunday morning dawned, videos showed jubilant scenes of citizens celebrating the overthrow of the Assad government in Aleppo, Homs, and the capital city of Damascus. Crowds gathered in Umayyad Square to topple the statue of Hafez al-Assad that David had seen every time he met Bashar over the years as he was driven to the Rowda Building.

Later in the day a source at the Kremlin announced that Bashar al-Assad had stepped down as president and fled with his family to Moscow where he was given asylum based on humanitarian grounds. According to the *Washington Post*, Syrian prime minister Mohammad Ghazi al-Jalali pledged cooperation with the rebel forces, noting that the opposition had promised "that they will not harm any person who belongs to the Syrian homeland."

Toppled statue of Hafez al-Assad, Damascus, December 2024

David followed the breaking news closely. Meetings in New York and Washington with UN and US State Department officials just a few weeks earlier had raised questions about Syria's stability. But the general consensus had been that its president was in control. David was familiar with the Islamist militant group HTS and had interviewed Syrian opposition fighters with ties to the group in 2014, during the civil war that by 2024 seemed to have all but ended. Now it appeared that the international experts had overestimated the strength of the Assad government. Al-Jolani, who led the HTS rebel offensive, was forty-two years old. Formerly affiliated with al-Qaeda and later the splinter group Jabhat al-Nusra, it appeared that over the last decade he had moved away from his jihadist views toward moderation, even using his real name, Ahmed al-Sharaa, in public. During the first days of the government takeover, he reassured panicked residents and foreign aid groups that "HTS wants to protect all government and international institutions serving the Syrian people, including

Liberated Syrian prison, January 2025

the United Nations." Would his reassurances hold? Could this new leader, who had discarded his jihadist military attire in favor of a more Western-style wardrobe, be trusted?

David's colleague Geir Pedersen, the UN's special envoy for Syria, told the *Washington Post* that the ousting of Assad "marks a watershed moment in Syria's history—a nation that has endured nearly 14 years of relentless suffering and unspeakable loss." Other figures on the international stage also commented on the historic events underway in Syria as the end of 2024 approached. Mazloum Abdi, commander-in-chief of the Syrian Democratic Forces, a Kurdish-led alliance, noted that "this change represents an opportunity to build a new Syria based on democracy and justice that guarantees the rights of all Syrians." Syrian state television went so far as to say that "the great Syrian revolution has succeeded, and the criminal regime of Assad has fallen."

"It is definitely a reshuffling of the deck that has defined Syria for twenty-four years of Bashar's presidency," David observes. As news poured in about the dramatic fall of Assad, global reactions were strong and mostly united. Syria's foreign ministry released a statement asserting that Syria would remain "committed to serving all fellow citizens," promising that the country's future would be one in which "justice and equality prevail." Speaking at a diplomatic forum in Qatar, Turkey's Minister of Foreign Affairs Hakan Fidan said that "as of this morning, Syria has reached a stage where the Syrian people will shape the future of their own country. Today there is hope." And according to the Associated Press, Daniel B. Shapiro, the US deputy assistant secretary of defense for the Middle East urged all parties "to protect civilians," adding that if the fall of Assad's regime is confirmed, "no one should shed any tears."

In the days that followed, more details of the seismic changes in Syria were revealed. On December 21 the *New York Times* published "Deception and Betrayal: Inside the Final Days of the Assad Regime," a lengthy article by Ben Hubbard, Farnaz Fassihi, Christina Goldbaum, and Hwaida Saad that captured the intrigue, twists, and turns of the factions and the continuing drama of a country on a new, uncertain trajectory. Hubbard, Goldbaum, and Saad traveled to Damascus from their bureaus in various countries in the Middle East and interviewed insiders in Assad's fallen government, as well as Iranian, Iraqi, and Turkish officials and rebels who participated in Assad's defeat.

According to the reporters, "many spoke on the condition of anonymity, citing diplomatic protocols, fear of retribution from remnants of the former regime—or from the rebels who toppled it." Fear of speaking openly had long plagued Syria's citizens, but now diverse perspectives helped piece together a remarkable tapestry of stories that had unfolded at lightning speed in the early weeks of December. Assad's former allies—Iran, Russia, and Iraq—could not or would not assist the Syrian president, and his army offered little resistance. In fact, many of its soldiers quickly changed from their uniforms into civilian clothes and fled the fighting. No one could really blame them. Many had been brought into the army by forced conscription, and economic distress in Syria reduced soldiers' salaries to less than $30 per month, an amount and lifestyle not worth fighting for.

Media around the world gave viewers and readers glimpses of the looting of the presidential palace, where David had been welcomed by Syria's First Lady during the early days of Assad's presidency. Photographs of defaced monuments, posters with Assad's image torn to pieces, and live coverage of reporters entering some of the country's most horrific prisons provided a startling real-time record of events. Television audiences saw political detainees and others freed from underground cells, some experiencing daylight for the first time in years, burst into tears caught on cameras for the world to see. There was hope again for answers about missing journalist Austin Tice. Early reports surfaced that new information was forthcoming as the Assad regime unraveled.

David sums up this unraveling in four words: "Assad waited too long." He explains that Assad and his inner circle always believed they had more leverage than they did and, perhaps more importantly, that time was on their side. "They thought conditions would eventually change in their favor and they could wait out any sticky situation. It could be the change in a US administration, a change in fortunes in the region that had nothing to do with anything Damascus did, or simply the passage of time." He had witnessed Assad's strategy of waiting out a crisis many times in the past. When former Lebanese prime minister Rafic Hariri was assassinated in 2005 and Syria was blamed by much of the Western world, David visited Damascus and observed that Assad waited for the international outcry to subside and that there were no consequences for him or his regime.

Time proved to be on his side again when his government was invited to participate in Arab-Israeli peace talks in the United States in 2007, despite the Bush administration's vehement opposition to him in 2003 when the United States was fighting in Iraq. David watched this "sense of triumphalism" serve Assad well over the many years he interacted with the Syrian president and as recently as 2023 it worked again. According to David, "Assad came out from the cold once again, when Syria was readmitted to the Arab League in May, after more than a decade of suspension, and a number of Arab countries reestablished diplomatic relations with Damascus. European countries began to engage with Syria, hoping a level of cooperation might help relieve the politically volatile issue of Syrian refugees in Europe. Even Turkish president Recep Tayyip Erdoğan, who had been the opposition's most avid supporter during the heyday of the Syrian civil war, made public overtures to Assad for a diplomatic rapprochement between the two countries.

"But Assad waited too long," David repeats. "He did not follow through on his promises made to Arab League countries, especially with regard to stemming Syria's drug trade. And even in the weeks before his fall, he did not give in to back-channel US offers to help facilitate the lifting of crippling international sanctions in return for a Syrian break with a weakened Iran and Hezbollah." Israel's relentless military pressure had degraded Hamas and Hezbollah over the previous year. While Assad played a waiting game, the opposition forces did not. They saw their chance for action and boldly took it, and Syria's long wait for change was over. Of course, what that change will mean in the years ahead is still to be determined.

On December 8, 2024, the Assad family flew to Moscow from a Russian airbase in Latakia, the coastal town David had visited during his student days. He remembered being there, in 1989, and the group of friendly young Russian sailors who orchestrated a night of fun in a bar near the harbor. Russia had offered the Assads safe haven. Asma's parents joined them there, traveling from London with the knowledge that they had become pariahs in the city that had been home for more than fifty years. Life had become insufferable in recent years as public revelations of the darkest sides of their son-in-law's governance surfaced. David knew another reason for their move: Asma had been diagnosed with a rare form of leukemia, a serious illness that she confronted after beating breast cancer in recent years. Now she would begin treatment in Moscow.

During the last weeks of 2024, David was a frequent guest on television and radio programs in the United States and abroad. They recognized his deep knowledge of Syria's history and his unique perspective on the man who had been unmasked as a monster to the world at large. He made appearances on ABC News, the BBC, the CBC, Finnish TV, CNBC, France 24, and Iraqi-Kurdish state television. He conducted interviews with newspapers and podcast hosts from around the globe. And all of these activities altered his year-end holiday plans dramatically. Judy's understanding of her husband's ability to respond to unexpected challenges eased his guilt about a grueling travel schedule. She encouraged him during this remarkable calendar of commitments, knowing that David could provide a thoughtful analysis of one of the Middle East's most important moments in recent history.

For weeks he covered the unfolding drama for the media, reminding the public that "Syria's status quo had become a dilapidated economy that had suffered from over a decade of war, withering sanctions, government neglect, rapacious warlords, and even more corruption than that which existed before the civil war." In his view, "The Syrian government had become a car without an engine, stuck and unable to move. Life for most Syrians—all but the privileged few—had severely deteriorated." The country's long-awaited change was a product of Syrian desperation.

> Bashar al-Assad was called "the hope" in Syria even before he became president in 2000, as many in and outside of the country were hoping he would be a breath of fresh air. Early in his time in power this hope seemed possible when he enacted some policies and indicated he might make some reforms to the stultifying Syrian system. But that quickly gave way to business as usual in Syria. He assimilated into the system and the system changed him. In the end, Syrians lost all hope, even among many of his supporters. They were not going to protect a rusting, decaying old car. Anything would be better. There will be no more opportunities for Bashar al-Assad.

Calling on his decades of experience in Syria, David prepared a number of memos for UN and government officials suggesting ways Syria might move forward in a positive direction. In early January, at David's urging, Gerry McHugh and Conflict Dynamics International compiled a list of lessons learned from previous similar situations of transition in Sudan, South Sudan, and Serbia, and David forwarded it to pertinent officials:

- **Role of military.** A critical consideration in the early stages post transition is the role of military actors in executive governance arrangements. If military actors have sole or veto-based decision-making influence in transitional executive arrangements, it could delay or obstruct subsequent civilian governance, especially within the executive.

- **Sufficient consensus with essential actors.** There is a honeymoon period following a sudden transition, especially because different groupings will still be willing to contribute to a broad-based configuration. If a power vacuum persists, different constituencies may seek to stake out more extreme or polarizing positions as a means of gaining (perceived) leverage. It is important to get minimal sufficient agreement between *essential* Syrian actors quickly. (An example is Sudan's engagement of all parties to draft its Constitutional Declaration in 2019.)

- **Short initial foundational document.** Any agreed approaches now need to be broad (on constituencies) and shallow (on detail). A "Statement of Agreed Actions" type of document (short; 3 to 6 pages) can set out the main agreed parameters quickly in terms of transitional governance arrangements and immediate process steps. (An example is the "Preceding Points Document" implemented by Serbia and Montenegro in 2003.)

- **Focus on what is achievable.** Any transitional governance arrangements and political processes should not try to take on too much in too short a period of time; that will result in unmet expectations. The mantra now for emergent Syrian leaders should be "under promise and over deliver." (An example is the ARCSS Agreement in South Sudan in 2015.)

- **Resist special provisions now.** Any actions for region-specific special transitional arrangements should not be considered bilaterally as that generally obstructs more national processes later. (Examples are the Kurdish Regional Authority in Iraq TAL in 2004 and the Darfur Regional Authority in Sudan in 2006.)

- **Formal civil society role.** It can be helpful to formalize civil society constituency roles—e.g., in a Transitional Legislative Council—otherwise there is the risk of elite-based deals that exclude other constituencies.

Syrian president Ahmed al-Sharaa meeting with Turkish president Recep Tayyip Erdoğan in Istanbul, May 25, 2025

As Syria prepared its new face for the world at large, news coverage presented scenarios that might emerge, and diplomats, government officials, and other international agencies and NGOs offered to come to the discussion table. David was invited by the Harmoon Center for Contemporary Studies to visit Damascus in July 2025 as keynote speaker at an international conference. Memories of the many times he had traveled there during the decades of Assad leadership flooded over him. As he prepared to return to what was being touted as a new Syria, he wondered what he would hear from new leadership and prepared to listen.

Meanwhile on May 14 President Donald Trump met with Syrian President Ahmed al-Sharaa in Riyadh, Saudia Arabia, after announcing his intention to lift sanctions against Syria the day before. It was the first meeting between leaders of the United

States and Syria in 25 years and President Trump described President al-Sharaa as a "young, attractive guy with a very strong past" and the Syrian leader expressed his willingness to eventually join the Abraham Accords, a US-brokered agreement between Israel and several Arab states. When President Trump announced that he planned to lift comprehensive sanctions against Syria, David recognized the enormous impact this decision will have. "This is a godsend to the Syrian government," he says, "as the country's economy has shrunk by more than 85 percent since the beginning of the civil war in 2011, while 90 percent of the population is living in poverty. The government of President Ahmed al-Sharaa has no chance of establishing stability, or even staying in power, unless it can grow the economy and turn those statistics around. The lifting of sanctions will allow for international investment in Syria's reconstruction as well as integration into the global financial system again, all of which is necessary for the Syrian government to integrate the plethora of militias and armed groups into a national military that can establish overall security to the country. This had very little chance of happening without the lifting of US sanctions."

He explains that there exists a very complex web of international sanctions that have been placed on Syria over the last four decades, including that country's presence on the original list issued by the US State Department in 1979 of state sponsors of terrorism. A slew of additional sanctions followed when the Syrian uprisings and civil war broke out in 2011, against institutions including the Central Bank of Syria, as well as political, military, and business leaders associated with the Assad regime. And in 2019, Congress passed the Caesar Act, a sweeping bill composed of secondary sanctions in the wake of atrocities purportedly committed by the Assad government. The EU and UN also enacted sanctions against Syria, and according to David, all of this will take years to untangle in any official manner.

"In the interim, it is likely that the White House will issue executive orders waiving the enforcement of US sanctions," David says, "and while it will take some time for the average Syrians to notice a significant difference in their everyday lives, some positive movement already has occurred. The Syrian pound rose very soon after President Trump announced the lifting of sanctions, gasoline prices fell a bit, and countries and companies are now willing and openly negotiating reconstruction contracts with Syria now that they are free of the fear of crossing the US Treasury and subjecting themselves to secondary sanctions. No doubt there will be more surprises in Syria—perhaps positive ones—as this new drama unfolds."

Yonghun Kim, David Lesch, and former San Antonio mayor Ron Nirenberg, 2022

EPILOGUE

Soft lighting, a private corner table, and a gathering of diverse colleagues sharing important conversation and delicious food can create a space where camaraderie and solutions unite. In keeping with President Ronald Reagan's pronouncement that "all great change in America begins at the dinner table," David knows that shared meals generate ideas that can lead to substantive progress locally, nationally, and internationally. From the Capital Grille in Washington, DC, to Hakkasan in Abu Dhabi, to J-Prime Steakhouse in San Antonio, he regularly invites guests to join him for an evening where differences are left at the door and common ground is explored. Mutual respect and good food can be catalysts for positive changes in America and beyond.

As early as his election to the San Antonio city council, Ron Nirenberg began meeting with David, recognizing his links to the worlds of politics and government. When he became mayor of the country's seventh largest city in 2017, the meetings became more frequent. Nirenberg wanted to build the city's international presence, with both new business partnerships and additional "sister city" relationships. David had international contacts all over the world and was delighted to brainstorm about entrepreneurial ideas.

"David is at his core a connector," Nirenberg says. "He brings people together from a vast array of friendships that he has made from his time as an academic, diplomat, and athlete. He has an intuition about people that allows him to know who fits together. I've spent a lot of time with David at gatherings around a dinner table, meeting new people, sharing in-depth discussions about the state of affairs in our city and our bigger world." Nirenberg is impressed by David's access to an extraordinarily wide array of experts. "He will say, 'Oh you should meet this diplomat or this professional baseball player,' or whatever, and he picks up the phone, puts them on FaceTime, and suddenly I am talking to them. They all pick up the phone for David."

After Nirenberg met with David and Yonghun Kim to explore business relationships between San Antonio and South Korea that involve some of the largest Korean companies, a trip to Seoul was planned. The delegation included the mayor, the city's chief protocol officer Sherry Dowlatshahi, and several other officials and business leaders. When Nirenberg was whisked away to a karaoke bar by Kim, Dowlatshahi was a bit worried about the departure from her well-choreographed schedule. Nirenberg rose to the occasion, however, choosing an old Frank Sinatra song for his performance. He told the story with some humor but completely understood that it also reflected the multiple and sometimes unexpected components that are part of international relationships. That evening the common ground was music.

In sharp contrast, not long after he returned from South Korea, international relations took a more conflicted turn in San Antonio. Following the attack on Israel by Hamas in 2023 and the ensuing war in Gaza, pro-Palestine and pro-Israel protests took place at city hall. Nirenberg turned to David for insights about how to navigate the situation. He read David's books to understand the historical context and talked with diverse groups to hear multiple perspectives. "It is somewhat disturbing to realize that because everything today is televised and digitized, the opinions and rhetoric have gotten so strident, without a real underpinning of knowledgeable information. That's why I sought David's guidance. I found that the kind of objectivity that David portrays is undergirded by his knowledge of history, in all of its complexity. Just understanding that level of complexity is a public service, an important service to humanity really."

Nirenberg has seen San Antonio mature into a multicultural city recognized for its tolerance of the complexities that are part of the modern world. He outlined this evolution, and his role in its progression during the four terms he served as mayor, in *Nirenberg: The Education of a Public Servant*, a memoir that he coauthored with David, scheduled for publication in early 2026. Personal injury and civil litigation attorney Tim Maloney witnessed these changes as well, praising city leaders like Nirenberg and educators like David for "taking a sleepy town into the big time." Maloney also has made films and documentaries that explored serious CIA-like scenarios in international situations, realms that David has experienced firsthand and always an interesting topic of conversation for the two friends.

Maloney introduced David to Justin Hill, a trial lawyer in San Antonio who serves on the board of Restore Education, a nonprofit GED program that works to maximize students' potential for success through innovative education solutions. He also hosts a popular podcast, *The Alamo Hour*, highlighting people, places, and passions that impact the city, and on occasion, the world beyond. David has been a guest on the podcast, and Hill says the episode was one of the show's best. "David's worldview and knowledge base set him apart from anyone else I have run across in local politics or San Antonio in general," he says.

The attorney has called David a top power broker in San Antonio and was delighted to become part of his always-expanding brainstorming team, joining other local leaders to discuss how the city can increase its international footprint and deal with important local issues, ranging from exploring changes in San Antonio's city government structure to promoting new initiatives in education, technology development, and violence prevention. The impressive group of city leaders from diverse fields meets regularly to discuss strategy. Members include Graham Weston, Rackspace founder and education advocate; Lew Moorman, a guru for technology start-ups; Henry Flores, professor emeritus at St. Mary's University; April Ancira, the civic-minded vice president of the Ancira Auto Group; and Gordon Hartman, founder of Morgan's Wonderland and a powerful advocate for inclusiveness in all realms.

"David has a deep understanding of geopolitics and diplomacy that luckily is not being sequestered within his academic pursuits. Those qualities, along with his interpersonal skills, have allowed him to become an important local, national, and international voice," Justin Hill says, adding that David's charisma is a powerful presence at the dinner table or the conference table. "He can be the stuffy, high-minded academic in meetings with world leaders, but he has the unique ability to sit around with friends and be relaxed, personable, and hilarious as he discusses the whole spectrum of issues and ideas. He can fit any situation. That is one of the things that make him uniquely positioned to do whatever he chooses."

Alberto Garza, another member of the brainstorming team and David's longtime tennis buddy, agrees. Originally from Monterrey, Mexico, Garza moved to San Antonio twenty-five years ago and says David was his first "gringo" friend. A businessman who owns several companies focused on the sale and distribution of oil products, he and David have worked together on a variety

EPILOGUE   233

From left: Leo Gomez, Yonghun Kim, Ron Nirenberg, Rico Izaguirre (standing), and David Lesch, 2021

of entrepreneurial projects in Mexico, and more are in the idea stage. Garza echoes Maloney's and Hill's assessments of their friend, using descriptors like "brilliant," "passionate," and "kind." Oliver Lee, founder and president of IronSight Capital and a trustee of Trinity University, and Juan Sepulveda, an endowed professor of political science at Trinity and head of the White House Initiative on Educational Excellence for Hispanics during the Obama administration, also belong to David's brainstorming group. They call David the "ultimate diplomat" and point to the variety of professions, political affiliations, and countries of origin present whenever they meet.

A particular episode of the television series *The Diplomat* resonates with David. The lead character, a prominent former diplomat, is giving a talk at Chatham House, a British think tank in

London. He says, "Talk to everyone. Talk to the dictator, the war criminal, terrorists. Talk to everyone, and fail and fail again, because maybe, just maybe...a breakthrough can be reached, but only by going down those difficult paths." David agrees that communication is key to international diplomacy and adds that the notion about giving "bad people" legitimacy by talking to them is nonsense. "More often than not, you give these people and groups more legitimacy by ignoring them."

One of David's favorite diplomacy stories dates to 2009, when he was invited to Israel to give a keynote address about Bashar al-Assad at Tel Aviv University and was scheduled to meet with a number of high-ranking government and military officials. Before leaving on the trip, David met with his longtime friend Imad Moustapha, the Syrian ambassador to the United States, in Washington, DC, to tell him about his travel plans. He asked Moustapha if the Syrian government had a message for him to carry to Benjamin Netanyahu, with whom David was scheduled to meet. Moustapha said there was no message. The ambassador said again, "I mean there is no message." David smiled and said he understood, although he was wondering why the ambassador had repeated himself. "No, you don't understand," Moustapha said. "The message is that there is NO message." David realized that it was actually an active, not passive, message. It meant "we have nothing to say to the Israelis."

David delivered his talk to a packed auditorium in Tel Aviv. During the question-and-answer period a reporter asked if David was carrying a message from President Assad to Israel's prime minister. He told the reporter he was not. Over the next few days he met with Israel's defense minister and former prime minister, Ehud Barak; President Shimon Peres; the chief of military intelligence, Amos Yadlin; and a host of other officials. But an hour before his scheduled meeting with Netanyahu, he learned the

EPILOGUE

meeting had been canceled. The prime minister had heard from a reporter that David might be carrying a message from Bashar and did not want to give the impression that he was meeting with someone who might be a messenger for the Syrian president. A month later David was in Syria and scheduled to meet with Bashar. Again his meeting was canceled at the last minute by Bashar's chief of staff who did not want it to appear that they had welcomed an intermediary carrying a message from the Israelis.

Fraught with misunderstanding and suspicion and the unwarranted personal inconveniences to David, the story reveals the deep distrust between Israel and Syria and the difficulties that accompany even the simplest communications. David calls it "ridiculous posturing, where important conversations do not take place for fear of giving the wrong impression or even taking the first step," adding that if "posturing" as a word or action did not exist, peace building would be a much more direct and successful exercise.

In a keynote speech in June 2024 entitled "Communication in an Age of Outrage," David told an audience of municipal information officials that conflict is essential to change, growth, and evolution and reminded them that some of the best decision-making has been the result of what academia calls productive collisions. He worries that a new "outrage culture" is growing, however, and with it, the inability of people to constructively interact with one another. Social media has encouraged increasing numbers to accept surface information too quickly, without critical analysis, fueling extremist positions. "Very few people really listen," he says, "and often we are talking past each other." He offers a number of "rules for the road" that work whether the destination is a successful treaty between warring nations or a mutual understanding between friends who differ in opinion.

1. Identify the problem and agree that all concerned are *problem solvers*.

2. Don't listen to respond; really hear what someone is saying.

3. Use empathy to connect with the speaker, even if you disagree.

4. Ask good questions or make trenchant observations based on what has been said.

5. Show respect and assure others that they have been heard.

6. Go to what William Ury calls the "balcony," a metaphor for stepping back and seeing the big picture of the situation.

7. Drill down to core issues; get past the bluster to find them.

8. Don't appear weak or strong; appear reasonable.

9. Brainstorm together without criticism or judgment.

10. Establish that everyone is in this together and there will be joint gain.

Both legitimate outrage and uninformed reactions to the war in Gaza in 2024 fueled emotions around the world. David saw the protests on US and European college campuses, and demonstrations at diverse locations—from federal buildings to music concerts to the Paris Olympics—and wondered how much the protest groups really understood about the profound issues behind the much-televised war. "There is plenty of blame to go around on all sides," he said in 2024, "but I am finding many protesters are being influenced by tendentious literature or speakers—not balanced information—sometimes merged with other issues including climate change and Black Lives Matter, creating a cauldron with far too many unrelated ingredients." He agrees with American commentator Thomas Friedman that "we cannot give Hamas 'a free pass' for what happened on October 7, but there is enough space to be both anti-Hamas and anti–Israeli policy."

On July 5, 2024, Keir Starmer was appointed prime minister of the United Kingdom. The next day in Damascus, Syrian presidential adviser Luna al-Shibl died as a result of a vehicle collision that some observers speculate was arranged for political reasons. On July 8 reformist Masoud Pezeshkian was elected president of Iran. In October Claudia Sheinbaum was sworn in as president of Mexico, and in November Donald Trump was elected president of the United States. January 2025 opened with Justin Trudeau's resignation as prime minister of Canada and closed with the appointment of Ahmed Al-Sharaa as the new president in Syria. This short sample of events, along with the scheduled elections in Israel in 2026, France in 2027, and in other countries, characterizes the recurring shifts in leadership across the globe and their interconnected impact on world affairs.

When former US president Jimmy Carter passed away at the age of one hundred on December 29, 2024, the world community reflected on his accomplishments and contributions while holding office and during his many years thereafter. International accolades poured in for a leader who had worked so hard for peace. Carter had read David's biography of Bashar al-Assad carefully before meeting with the Syrian president in 2009, and he read his subsequent books over the years, always sending a handwritten note of congratulations. As the former president's health failed, he read David's 2023 book *A History of the Middle East Since the Rise of Islam* and sent a message typed by his assistant. It included one of Carter's favorite mottos: "You talk to everyone, even your enemies, because after all, you don't need to make peace with your friends, only with those you oppose." David was inspired by Carter's many achievements, including the complicated peace-building challenges in the Middle East they experienced together, and by his genuine kindness. He joined the nation as it watched Carter's memorial service at the Washington

National Cathedral in early January 2025, attended by all five living presidents. Less than two weeks later, the country witnessed the inauguration of President Donald Trump, preparing to serve his second term.

In an opinion piece for *Manara Magazine*, published by the Cambridge Middle East and North Africa Forum in the UK in early December 2024, David suggested that Trump's election would prompt foreign policy changes. "President Trump's focus on 'the art of the deal' in his last administration saw a transactional foreign policy taking root," he wrote. According to David, this approach could lead to an expansion of the Abraham Accords, the series of bilateral agreements signed in 2020 during Trump's first term, that normalized relations between Israel and a host of Arab states. In an ideal situation the new administration would want to see that expansion include the normalization of relations between Israel and Saudi Arabia, something the Biden administration was working on when Hamas terrorists attacked Israel on October 7, 2023, effectively dooming its success. If Trump could bring about a Saudi-Israeli agreement, he would be able to tout the fact that he achieved something former president Biden could not.

"Trump's art of the deal approach may also impact the Iranian nuclear situation," David observed. "Trump is not against a deal with Iran per se. He has always said that he abrogated the JCPOA [Joint Comprehensive Plan of Action] because he thought it was a bad deal and that he could negotiate a better one." Diplomats in the know report that Iran has been sending signals that it may be ready to reach a deal with Trump, and when his unofficial adviser Elon Musk met with Iran's ambassador to the UN in New York shortly after the US election, the international community noticed.

"During Trump's prior term in the White House, there had

EPILOGUE

been no greater pro-Israeli president in US history," David said. "Remember that he moved the US embassy from Tel Aviv to Jerusalem and recognized Israeli sovereignty over the Golan Heights. And during the 2024 election campaign, he mentioned his support for Israel's potential annexation of the West Bank. It is not a secret that Israeli Prime Minister Benyamin Netanyahu and other officials of that government were hoping for Trump's election. But all sorts of new 'dealmaking' ideas are in the mix; the future of the entire region will be impacted in the years ahead."

Just a month before Assad's ouster in Syria, a *New Yorker* article, "How Syria Became the Middle East's Drug Dealer," by Ed Caesar described another troubling part of the Middle East story. As a result of that country's conflicts and shattered economy, illicit trade of the synthetic stimulant Captagon had become a big source of financial support for the Assad government. It had become popular during the civil war as a way to keep soldiers alert and "juiced up." According to Caesar, Bashar's younger brother Maher al-Assad, while head of the Fourth Armored Division of the Syrian Army, led the production and distribution of the drug, a type of amphetamine, that became a $10 billion business for Syria, with Saudi Arabia its biggest customer. He compares Syria's economic dependence on Captagon to the Bolivian government's reliance on the cocaine trade and to the way the Taliban stayed afloat thanks to its opium revenue during the years it was fighting US forces for control of Afghanistan. The drug was supposedly used by Saddam Hussein's army. Syrian fighters on all sides of the civil war have taken it, and Israel Defense Forces reported finding Captagon pills on the bodies of Hamas fighters killed during the October 7, 2023, attacks.

In the spring of 2024 Caesar traveled to Jordan to interview Samir Rifai, the country's former prime minister, for his article. David got to know Rifai well when they both were at Harvard's

Center for Middle Eastern Studies from 1984 to 1985, and both had followed the dramas in Syria for decades. Caesar and Rifai sat in the garden, gazing across the border to Israel and the West Bank. Jericho was just visible. Syria, to the north, was out of sight. As the two men talked, the region's interconnectivity must have been palpable. Rifai, like so many leaders in the Middle East, had felt dismay over neighboring Syria's declining situation. Just one month after Caesar's article was published, that situation changed in ways neither the author nor Rifai could have predicted on that lovely spring day in Jordan. Whether the Captagon trade will also change remains an open question today.

After returning from his first trip to Syria in 1989, David Lesch told his family and friends he had fallen in love with the country's remarkable history, cultures, and landscapes. That has not changed. "I would absolutely like to visit Syria again," David says wistfully, and he remains magnanimous about the different treatment he has received as a guest there.

> Of course, after my 2011 op-ed in the *New York Times* and my subsequent criticisms of the Syrian government and its policies during the civil war, I became persona non grata. And Bashar certainly did not like the title of my 2013 book, *The Fall of the House of Assad*, even though it predicted that he would most likely stay in power, for the time being, unlike some of the other Middle East leaders during the early days of the Arab Spring. When I visited Damascus that year, he would not see me during my meetings with Bouthaina Shaaban and Khaled al-Ahmad in the Rowda Building, just one floor below his office. However, when I was in Toronto for some mediation meetings in 2019, I received a call from a prominent Syrian interlocutor with Bashar who told me that Damascus wanted to build a relationship with me again. It was a very slow walk toward regaining access, but I met with Bashar's

father-in-law on a regular basis in London. That would not have happened without the president's consent. So I imagined I would return to Syria sometime in 2025 and would meet with Bashar again. I did not think we would ever again have the comfortable relationship we had prior to the civil war, but I was hopeful that it would be a respectful one where items of mutual US-Syrian concern could be discussed. I knew we had both changed over the years since I last saw him in 2009. I wondered if the violence and angst of the civil war had affected his worldview. Of course, now that meeting in Damascus will not happen.

Dan Goodgame, former editor of *Texas Monthly* and a former journalist in the Middle East, observed as a young journalist several decades ago, "One of the interesting things about Syria was it was just about impossible to get anyone to tell you anything useful while you were there. The best information you could get was from outside the country." This observation still holds true decades later. Most Syrian citizens kept their political views private under the Assads, and many subjects were simply not discussed.

Whispered stories about violent internal conditions surfaced but appeared to have become an accepted part of Syria's existence. Prior to the fall of the Assad government, human rights organizations, the UN, and international news sources identified more than twenty-seven prisons and detention centers around the country run by the Syrian government. An article by Anand Gopal, published on March 11, 2024, in *The New Yorker*, took readers inside Al-Hol ("the horror"), one of the country's most notorious detention camps.

Reports from Amnesty International concluded that the camp lived up to its name and that more than 50,000 people lived within the fenced open-air compound. Run by the Syrian

Democratic Forces and Kurdish military, not the government, it mostly held women and children thought to be part of the ISIS network. Other detention centers run by the Syrian government were known to hold prisoners perceived as opposing Bashar al-Assad. But none of the official reports prepared the world for what they saw when the prison cell doors were unlocked in December 2024 and images of starved and tortured prisoners and their underground holding pens flooded the news.

David sees the challenges for the new Syrian government as formidable. First and foremost, the new leaders will have to rebuild and restructure an economy corrupted by war, dominated by rapacious warlords, and devastated by extensive US-led international sanctions. The lifting or waiving of sanctions will depend on Syria's acquiring international approval of the type of nonsectarian, inclusive government that many countries, including the United States, want to see formed. Along these lines, the narco-state built up by Assad will have to be dismantled, which is a formidable task since organized crime syndicates with private militias are prevalent and many Syrians have become addicted to Captagon.

"Of course, there is the question of justice and accountability, trying to find the correct balance between overall reconciliation and restorative justice against those in the Assad regime," David explains, "and specific questions of property and housing, and as Syrian refugees return, what they will find." Competing factions with different alliances and agendas in the region complicate the country's restoration.

> There are the problems of what to do about the US-supported and
> Kurdish-dominated Syrian Democratic Forces in the northeast,
> the potential of a resurgent ISIS taking advantage of the vacuum
> of power created by Assad's fall, possible attempts by Iran to

EPILOGUE

243

destabilize what had been a reliable ally, and possible Israeli military expansion into the Golan Heights across the UN ceasefire lines established in 1974, as well as its continuing strikes against the former regime's weapons depots and military facilities that could fall into what it views as the wrong hands.

In 2025 intermediaries with access to the new leadership in Syria contacted David about a visit to Damascus, with the opportunity to lead one or two delegations. One would be with the Abraham Path Initiative to discuss reviving efforts to include Syria in the walking path project. The prospect is possible with a more inclusive and nonsectarian government eager to improve the image of the country and to boost the economy through tourism. Plans are also brewing for David and Gerry McHugh to visit in conjunction with broader UN efforts to assist with the country's transition from the Assad government to a new future.

F. Gregory Gause III says that his longtime friend is "an unusual combination of an excellent scholar and a very practical person who can get things done."

> In the academic world, one can find the one or the other but rarely together in one person. The challenge of restoring a Syria that is orderly, at a minimum, is great. A Syria that is not only orderly but decent toward its citizens and open to their talents is an even bigger challenge. No one person can bring that about, particularly folks from outside Syria. However, David can play an important role in connecting a restored and reformed Syria to the United States, both politically and economically, and in helping Washington understand how to help Syria get to that desired end state.

Garrett M. Graff, a historian and contributing columnist for the *Washington Post*, has identified these essential qualities for

David Lesch throwing the opening pitch at a Saraperos baseball game in Saltillo, Mexico

great leadership: integrity, vision, curiosity, lifelong learning, the ability to pivot and reinvent oneself, "a tolerance for voices far more varied than those of the past, and a willingness to bring people along." There is consensus from so many camps that David Lesch embodies these attributes and values, preparing him for continued success in a complicated world where history, politics, objectivity, and compassion merge.

A top political insider in Washington has suggested that, under the right conditions, David might be considered for the position of secretary of state. Admirers from all walks of life have urged him to run for office, and one patron has offered to finance a presidential campaign. David believes that project would be difficult because of the low public profile he has kept, but his political prospects are tantalizing. In the meantime, the unique journey of David Lesch continues.

Acknowledgments

Writing a biography is a wonderful endeavor when the main character is making positive contributions to the world and also happens to be a "nice guy" whose moral compass gives me hope for humankind. A combination of intelligence, compassion, and creativity makes David Lesch an important figure in the twenty-first century, and I'm grateful to him for choosing me as his biographer. I am doubly grateful for all the insights that his wife, Judy Dunlap, contributed to this story about one of the most unique people I have ever met. By the way, it was Judy who thought of the book's clever and inviting title.

This is the fourth book I have published with Trinity University Press, and I appreciate that talented team of professionals, with special thanks to John Gehner, who produced a careful copyedit for a book filled with historical facts and complex timelines and names. Crystal Hollis/Seale Studios created the eye-catching cover, graphically combining the disparate themes of baseball and the Middle East.

Curiosity about David's unique life journey and admiration for his innovative spirit led Trinity trustee Herb Stumberg to support this project with both creative ideas and financial backing. As the founder of the Louis H. Stumberg New Venture

Competition at Trinity, designed to inspire students to become future entrepreneurs, Stumberg recognized the extraordinary real-life adventures that have taken David from the pitcher's mound in professional baseball to hostage negotiations in the Middle East, from innovative approaches to the peace process in Syria to consultancies for international companies that stretch from Korea to Mexico. And, of course, Stumberg admired David's award-winning teaching and the crucial role it plays in preparing a younger generation for the challenges of the twenty-first century and beyond.

Speaking of the challenges facing our world, for more than five decades Peter C. Goldmark has been on the front line when it comes to searching for solutions, serving as president of the Rockefeller Foundation, chairman and CEO of the *International Herald Tribune*, and director of the climate and air program for the Environmental Defense Fund. His foreword to this book is inspirational and powerful, and I am grateful to be his friend.

Thanks to fascinating interviews with David's close friends, family members, colleagues from the worlds of democracy and academia, journalists, current and former students, and others, I was exposed to David's multifaceted character. The following individuals agreed to interviews, providing essential firsthand information and depth to this biography: Kamal Alam, a visiting fellow at the Royal United Services Institute in London and at the Atlantic Council in Washington, DC, and an expert on Syrian affairs with The Institute for Statecraft; Hrair Balian, former director of the Conflict Resolution Program at the Carter Center in Atlanta; Jeffrey Feltman, a fellow at the Brookings Institute and former under-secretary-general for political affairs at the UN, assistant secretary of state for Near Eastern affairs, and former US ambassador to Lebanon; F. Gregory Gause III, professor emeritus of international affairs at The Bush School of Government and

Public Service at Texas A&M University; Gerry McHugh, founder and head of Conflict Dynamics International; Ron Nirenberg, former mayor of San Antonio; and William Ury, founder of the Harvard Negotiation Project. Debra Tice, mother of journalist Austin Tice, who disappeared in Syria in 2012, shared her ongoing—and heart wrenching—efforts to obtain information about her son from the Syrian government and ways that David is helping her do that.

Dan Goodgame, former editor of *Texas Monthly* and a former journalist in the Middle East, reminisced about the historic intrigue in that region and shared memories of dodging the secret police to report a story. Tom Ewald, now an investment manager in Greenwich, Connecticut, described the drama of being taken hostage by Iraqi forces during the Gulf War, and how he contacted David—his former professor at Harvard—when he was released by Saddam Hussein. Robert Freedman, a political scientist who held appointments at Baltimore Hebrew University and Johns Hopkins University, taught David at the University of Maryland, Baltimore County and encouraged him to pursue graduate degrees at Harvard. John McCusker, retired Ewing Halsell Distinguished Professor of History at Trinity University, explained the complex world of academia to me and the brilliant way David climbed the competitive ladder at the university. Vanessa Beasley, president of Trinity University, added her insights about David's long teaching career and the impact he has had on his students.

Tom Kayser, who served as president of the Texas League for twenty-five years, gave me a crash course in Baseball 101. Childhood friends Doug Reitz and Kevin Birchen told me stories about David's incredible athletic prowess, coupled with a "kindness factor" that made him unique. Former students Joe Balat, Rico Izaguirre, Jackie Montaine, Ansel Stein, Kevin Stryker, and Jacob

Uzman told me how their professor had changed their lives and prepared them for the interesting things they do today as adults making a difference in the world.

Ahmad Zahra, a Syrian-American filmmaker and city councilman in California, and longtime friend of David's, visited Damascus in early 2024 after more than a decade without seeing family and friends living in Syria. His firsthand descriptions of the landscapes there, both physical and human, were immensely helpful, and he contributed some of the beautiful photographs that appear in this book.

Family members were also immensely helpful. David's brother Robert (Bob) Lesch recounted childhood adventures and David's unique can-do spirit, and as mentioned before, his wife Judy Dunlap provided important glimpses into David's more personal side.

A special member of my own family was my rock during this two-year project. My husband, Geary Atherton, a graduate in political science from Stanford University, read every draft and allowed me long hours to write while cheerfully taking on many of my daily tasks. Partnership makes such a difference in life. I am truly blessed.

IMAGE CREDITS

Unless otherwise noted, images are courtesy of the David Lesch Photo Collection.

page 8, Alamy
page 12, Alamy
page 22, Courtesy of Joan K. Cooke
page 30, *Baltimore Sun*
page 47, Alamy
page 56, *Baltimore Sun*
page 58, *Boston Globe*
page 65, Alamy
page 67, Alamy
page 72, Courtesy of Ahmad Zahra
page 81, Courtesy of Trinity University
page 88, Alamy
page 92, Courtesy of Ahmad Zahra
page 102, Alamy
page 110, Alamy
page 112, Courtesy of Ahmad Zahra
page 123, Courtesy of Ahmad Zahra
page 134, Courtesy of Ahmad Zahra

IMAGE CREDITS

page 151, Alamy

page 158, Alamy

page 160, Alamy

page 164, Courtesy of Debra and Marc Tice

page 177, Alamy

page 184, Alamy

page 194, Courtesy of Ahmad Zahra

page 214, Alamy

page 217, Alamy

page 218, Alamy

page 225, Alamy

BIBLIOGRAPHY

PRIMARY SOURCES

Interviews with David W. Lesch
Correspondence, personal scrapbooks, and photographs of David W.
    Lesch
Photo collection of Ahmad Zahra

INTERVIEWS AND SURVEYS CONDUCTED BY THE AUTHOR, NOVEMBER 2022 TO JUNE 2024

Kamal Alam, Joseph Balat, Hrair Balian, Vanessa Beasley, Kevin Birchen, Bill Clover, Judy Dunlap, Tom Ewald, Jeffrey Feltman, Robert Freedman, Alberto Garza, F. Gregory Gause III, Dan Goodgame, Justin Hill, Ulrico Izaguirre, Tom Kayser, Oliver Lee, Bob Lesch, David Lesch, Tim Maloney, John McCusker, Jackie Montaine, Ron Nirenberg, Doug Reitz, Juan Sepulveda, Ansel Stein, Kevin Stryker, Herb Stumberg, Debra Tice, William Ury, Jacob Uzman, Ahmad Zahra.

PUBLICATIONS

Alam, Kamal. "Kissinger's Prophecy Fulfilled in Syria." *War on the Rocks*, January 23, 2019. https://warontherocks.com/2019/01 /kissingers-prophecy-fulfilled-in-syria.
Alam, Kamal, and David Lesch. "The Road to Damascus: The Arabs March Back to Befriend Assad." *War on the Rocks*, December 7, 2018.

https://warontherocks.com/2018/12/the-road-to-damascus-the
-arabs-march-back-to-befriend-assad.

Arundel, John. "A Hostage Returns from the Persian Gulf." *New York
Times*, November 4, 1990. https://www.nytimes.com/1990/11/04
/nyregion/connecticut-q-a-thomas-hart-benton-ewald-a-hostage
-returns-from-the-persian-gulf.html.

Balian, Hrair, and Jeffrey Feltman. "The United States Needs a New
Syria Policy." *Responsible Statecraft*, January 20, 2021. https://
responsiblestatecraft.org/2021/01/20/the-united-states-needs
-a-new-syria-policy.

Balian, Hrair, and George A. Lopez. "An Opportunity to Energize
Multinational Diplomacy on Syria." *Responsible Statecraft*,
September 21, 2021. https://responsiblestatecraft.org/ 2021/09/21/
an-opportunity-to-energize-multinational-diplomacy-on-syria.

Bell, Gertrude. *The Desert and the Sown: The Syrian Adventures of the
Female Lawrence of Arabia*. Cooper Square Press, 2001.

Buck, Joan Juliet. "The Rose of the Desert." *Vogue*, February 2011.

Caesar, Ed. "How Syria Became the Middle East's Drug Dealer." *New
Yorker*, November 4, 2024. https://www.newyorker.com/magazine
/2024/11/11/how-syria-became-the-middle-easts-drug-dealer.

Cafiero, Giorgio. "Debating the US Presence in Syria: The ISIS
Factor." *Responsible Statecraft*, February 12, 2024. https://
responsiblestatecraft.org/us-troops-in-syria.

Denny, Mary. "Middle East Expert Lesch Draws on Relationship with
Syrian President for Book." *Trinity*, Spring 2006.

El-Amine, Zein. *Is This How You Eat a Watermelon?* Radix Media, 2022.

Falle, Sam. *My Lucky Life: In War, Revolution, Peace, and Diplomacy*.
Book Guild, 1996.

Fisher, Roger, William Ury, and Bruce Patton. *Getting to Yes:
Negotiating Agreement Without Giving In*. Penguin Books, 2011.

Freedman, Robert O. *The Middle East Since Camp David*. Westview
Press, 1984.

Garcia, Victor. "Seminar Speaker Says Israelis, Arabs to Meet in
Washington." *San Antonio Express-News*, February 27, 1994.

Gause, F. Gregory, III. "The Price of Order: Settling for Less in the
Middle East." *Foreign Affairs*, March/April 2022. https://www
.foreignaffairs.com/middle-east/price-order.

BIBLIOGRAPHY

Gause, F. Gregory, III. "Should We Stay or Should We Go: The United States and the Middle East." *Survival: Global Politics and Strategy* 61, no. 6 (2019): 7–24. https://doi.org/10.1080/00396338.2019.1662114.

Georges, Christopher J., and Michael W. Hirschorn. "Prof Took 2nd CIA Grant." *Harvard Crimson*, October 11, 1985. https://www.thecrimson.com/article/1985/10/11/prof-took-2nd-cia-grant-pa.

Gopal, Anand. "The Open-Air Prison for ISIS Supporters—And Victims." *New Yorker,* March 11, 2024. https://www.newyorker.com/magazine/2024/03/18/the-open-air-prison-for-isis-supporters-and-victims.

Graff, Garrett M. "Great Leaders Are Scarce. How Do We Increase the Supply?" *Washington Post*, July 3, 2024. https://www.washingtonpost.com/opinions/2024/07/03/graff-leadership-curiosity-patience.

Haas, Mark L., and David W. Lesch, eds. *The Arab Spring: Change and Resistance in the Middle East.* Westview Press, 2012.

Hubbard, Ben, Farnaz Fassihi, Christina Goldbaum, and Hwaida Saad. "Deception and Betrayal: Inside the Final Days of the Assad Regime." *New York Times,* December 21, 2024. https://www.nytimes.com/2024/12/21/world/middleeast/assad-regime-syria-final-days.html.

Khalek, Renia. "Meet the Mystery Fixer Who Negotiated Syria out of Seven Years of War." *The Grayzone*, August 2, 2018. https://thegrayzone.com/2018/08/02/meet-the-mystery-fixer-who-negotiated-syria-out-of-seven-years-of-war.

Lesch, David W. *1979: The Year That Shaped the Modern Middle East.* Westview Press, 2001.

Lesch, David W. *The Arab-Israeli Conflict: A History*. 2nd ed. Oxford University Press, 2019.

Lesch, David W. "Be Careful What You Wish For, Mr. Netanyahu." *Manara Magazine*, December 6, 2024. https://manaramagazine.org/2024/12/be-careful-what-you-wish-for-mr-netanyahu.

Lesch, David W. "City Needs to Nurture International Ties." *San Antonio Express-News*, June 20, 2017.

Lesch, David W. "Failure of Soviets Can Teach America." *Dallas Morning News*, September 23, 2001.

Lesch, David W. *A History of the Middle East Since the Rise of Islam.* Oxford University Press, 2023.

Lesch, David W. "Invite Syria into the Diplomatic Circle." *San Antonio Express-News*, August 6, 2006.

Lesch, David W. "Iran Is Taking Over Syria. Can Anyone Stop It?" *New York Times,* August 29, 2017. https://www.nytimes.com/2017/08/29/opinion/iran-syria.html.

Lesch, David W. *The New Lion of Damascus: Bashar al-Asad and Modern Syria*. Yale University Press, 2005.

Lesch, David W. "Prevention Must Have Groundwork." *San Antonio Express-News*, September 14, 2001.

Lesch, David W. *Syria: A Modern History*. Polity Press, 2019.

Lesch, David W. *Syria: The Fall of the House of Assad*. Yale University Press, 2012.

Lesch, David W. *Syria and the United States: Eisenhower's Cold War in the Middle East*. Westview Press, 1992.

Lesch, David W. "The Syrian President I Know." *New York Times*, March 29, 2011. https://www.nytimes.com/2011/03/30/opinion/30lesch.html.

Lesch, David W. "Syrian Threat to Israel Not as Reported." *San Antonio Express-News*, November 12, 1996.

Lesch, David W. "The United States in the Middle East: An Historical Inquiry." *Texas Committee on US-Arab Relations Newsletter*, April 1994.

Lesch, David W., and James Gelvin. "Assad Has Won in Syria. But Syria Hardly Exists." *New York Times,* January 11, 2017. https://www.nytimes.com/2017/01/11/opinion/assad-has-won-in-syria-but-syria-hardly-exists.html.

Lesch, David W., and Mark L. Haas, eds. *The Middle East and the United States: History, Politics, and Ideologies*. Westview Press, 2011.

Lesch, David W., Frida Nome, George Saghir, William Ury, and Matt Waldman. "Obstacles to a Resolution of the Syrian Conflict." *Norwegian Institute for International Affairs*, November 2013. https://nupi.brage.unit.no/nupi-xmlui/handle/11250/276507.

Lesch, David W., and William Ury. "Dignity Key to Syria's Future." *CNN*, May 12, 2015. https://www.cnn.com/2015/05/12/middleeast/lesch-ury-syria-dignity.

Lesch, David W., and William Ury. "Syria and the Abraham Path Initiative: The Intersection of Religion and Tourism with Domestic and Regional Politics." Centre for Syrian Studies Papers, University of St. Andrews, 2026.

BIBLIOGRAPHY   *255*

Pearlman, Wendy. *We Crossed a Bridge and It Trembled: Voices from Syria*. HarperCollins, 2017.

Polk, William R. *The Opening of South Lebanon, 1788–1840: A Study of the Impact of the West on the Middle East.* Harvard University Press, 1963.

Posnanski, Joe. *Why We Love Baseball: A History in 50 Moments.* Penguin Random House, 2023.

Riedel, Bruce. "30 Years after Our 'Endless Wars' in the Middle East Began, Still No End in Sight." *Brookings Institution*, July 27, 2020. https://www.brookings.edu/articles/30-years-after-our-endless -wars-in-the-middle-east-began-still-no-end-in-sight.

Smagin, Nikita. "Moscow's Original 'Special Operation': Why Russia Is Staying in Syria." *Carnegie Politika*, February 7, 2023. https:// carnegieendowment.org/russia-eurasia/politika/2023/01/moscows -original-special-operation-why-russia-is-staying-in-syria?.

Sultan, Aisha, and Leila Merrill. "Middle East Conference Draws International Brain Power to Trinity." *Trinitonian*, March 3, 1994.

Trofimov, Yaroslav, and Sune Engel Rasmussen. "In the Conflict Between the West and Authoritarian Foes, Islamic State Sees All Sides as Targets." *Wall Street Journal*, March 23, 2024. https://www .wsj.com/world/middle-east/in-the-conflict-between-the-west-and -authoritarian-foes-islamic-state-sees-all-sides-as-targets-4e7277f3.

Ury, William. *Possible: How We Survive (and Thrive) in an Age of Conflict.* Harper Business, 2024.

Yacoubian, Mona. "Assad Is Here to Stay." *Foreign Affairs*, January 25, 2022. https://www. foreignaffairs.com/articles/middle-east/2022-01 -25/assad-here-stay.

INDEX

Page numbers followed by f indicate a figure or graphic.

Aberdeen Proving Ground, 12f, 12–13

Abraham, 6

Abraham Path Initiative (API), 138, 142, 150, 151
  Bashar al-Assad and, 139–40
  birth of the idea of, 137–38
  David and, 138, 139, 141, 143, 150, 151
  William Ury and, 137–39, 141, 143, 149

Abu Kamal raid (2008), 150–51

Ahmad, Khaled al-, 2, 173, 174

Alam, Kamal, 196–97

Alawites, 101–2

Aleppo, Syria, 175–77

Al-Hamidiyah (souk in Damascus), 194f

Al-Hol refugee camp, 241–42

Al-Nusra Front (Jabhat al-Nusra), 167–69

American Historical Association conference in Chicago (1992), 78, 79

Antakya, Turkey, 75

Anthony, John Duke, 98

Antioch, Turkey, 75, 76

Arab League, 165, 221

Arab Spring, 145, 160f, 160–61, 204

Arabian Desert, 1. *See also* Syrian Desert

Arab-Israeli conflict, 42, 129, 191, 202, 238. *See also* Israel-Syria relations; Israeli-Palestinian conflict
  George H. W. Bush and, 95
  Syria and, 103, 107–8, 121, 139, 140

Arafat, Yasser, 83–84

Arizona, 22f
  David in, 21, 23–24, 26–27

Armey, Dick, 122–23

Assad, Asma (Fawaz) al- (Bashar's wife), 127, 161
  background, 3, 124–26
  Bashar and, 3, 125–26, 126f, 159
  characterization of, 126–27
  David and, 125–27, 126f
  in Moscow, 222
  photographs, 126f, 127f, 159, 161

Assad, Bashar al-, 131–32, 242
Abraham Path Initiative (API) and, 139–40
Asma al-Assad and, 3, 125–26, 126f, 159
characterizations of, 120–23, 191, 223
David and, 99, 112, 128, 130–33, 131f, 139, 234
interviews and other meetings, 99, 114f, 115–20, 117f, 122–24, 128, 130–32, 139–40, 143–45, 150, 192, 204
David on, 122, 132, 218, 221
The New Lion of Damascus: Bashar al-Asad and Modern Syria, 3, 62, 124, 142, 237
"The Syrian President I Know" (Lesch), 162
and the death of his brother Bassel, 103–4
Donald Trump's letter to, 201
downfall. *See* Assad regime, fall of the
early life, 119–21, 124, 192
exile in Moscow, 216, 222
family, 125, 127, 127f, 161, 192. *See also* Assad family
Hafez al-Assad and, 2–3, 118–19, 121, 122, 129, 162
historical perspective on, 223
inaugural speech, 109
Iran and, 178, 204, 219, 221
Israel and, 121, 234
Jimmy Carter and, 149–51, 151f, 237
Lebanon and, 119, 122, 129, 178, 204
in London, 99, 103, 116, 120–21

office in Rowda Building, 115, 118, 119, 140
in Paris, 159
personality, 119, 120, 122, 123, 125–26, 128, 129, 132, 179, 191, 192, 221, 244
personality change, 129, 132, 223
photographs, 102f, 114f, 117f, 127f, 131f
reelection (2007), 131f, 131–32
rise to power, 103–4, 108–9, 112, 113, 118–19, 129
Russia and, 219, 222
United States and, 221
waiting games/strategy of waiting out a crisis, 220–21
Assad, Bassel al-, 103–4
Assad, Hafez al-, 62, 115
background, 101–2
Bashar and, 2–3, 118–19, 121, 122, 129, 162
characterization of, 204
death, 2, 108
Israel and, 117
Lebanon and, 53, 119
photographs, 102f, 117
presidency, 3, 62, 64, 101, 103, 107, 121, 169
Saddam Hussein and, 64, 65f, 71
seizing power, 101–3
toppled statue of, 216, 217f
United States and, 75, 94
Assad, Hafez Bashar al- (Bashar's son), 125, 127f, 161
Assad, Maher al- (Bashar's brother), 102f, 239
Assad, Rifaat al- (Hafez's brother), 103
Assad family, 101–2, 102f, 222. *See also* Assad, Bashar al-: family

INDEX

Assad regime, fall of the, 159–62, 168, 169, 214f, 215–23. *See also* Syrian revolution and civil war
  Arab Spring and, 145, 160f, 160–61, 204
  Iran and, 216, 219
  and the media, 159–63

Ba'ath Party, 64, 108, 118
Ba'athist Syrian Captagon industry, 189, 221, 239, 240, 242
Baker, James, 201–2
Balat, Joe, 97, 100, 107
Balian, Hrair
  background, 149, 190
  at Carter Center, 149, 152
  on conflict resolution, 190
  David and, 152–53, 176–77, 190
  on Gaza war, 190–91
  Jimmy Carter and, 152
  Lebanon and, 149, 176–77, 190, 191
  Syria and, 152, 176–77, 191
Baltimore Orioles, 28, 44
Barakat, Ghias, 113, 140, 142
Beasley, Vanessa, 212f, 212–13
Beirut
  barracks bombings (1983) in, 47
  siege of Beirut, 45–46
  US embassy bombing (1983) in, 47, 47f
Bel Air, Maryland
  David and, 4, 10
  Lesch family in, 10, 13, 30, 36f, 37, 57, 105–6, 180
Berkley, Shelley, 123
Bhutto, Benazir, 130f, 131
Biden, Joe, 209
  and the Tices, 199–202
Birchen, Kevin, 14–15

Blais, Maxine (Suzanne's mother), 68, 70
Blumenthal, Sidney, 163
Bolton, John, 199–200
Bouazizi, Mohamed, 160
Brewers. *See* Milwaukee Brewers
Brooke Army Medical Center, 130
Brzezinski, Zbigniew, 43, 52–53
Buck, Joan Juliet, 161
Burns, Tom, 39–40
Bush, George H. W., 77, 94–96, 106
Bush, George W.
  David and, 106, 121–22
  9/11 terrorist attacks and, 110–11
  Syria and, 121–22

Cable News Network (CNN), 53–54
Caesar Syria Civilian Protection Act of 2019 (Caesar Act), 226
Cairo, 48–49
Calgaard, Ron, 79–80, 86f
Camp David Accords, 25. *See also* Egypt-Israel peace treaty
Cantori, Louis, 39, 41, 43–46, 48–49
Cantú García, César H., 209–10, 210f
Carew, Rod, 28
Carter, Jimmy, 25, 149–52
  Bashar al-Assad and, 149–51, 151f, 237
  David and, 150, 151, 237–38
  death, 237
  William Ury and, 136, 149
Carter Center, 26, 149, 152
Central Arizona College, 21, 23, 26–32
Central Intelligence Agency (CIA). *See* CIA funding
Cey, Ron, 8
CIA funding, Nadav Safran's, 58f, 59, 61, 62

Clinton, Bill, 107–8
Clinton, Hillary, 163
Clover, Williston, 82
"Communication in an Age of Out-
    rage" (Lesch's keynote), 235
Constitution of Ba'athist Syria (1973),
    102
Coolidge, Arizona, 23–24
Corrective Movement (1970 coup), 101
Crichton, Flora Cameron, 86, 94
Cure Violence, 200

Dalai Lama, 128
Dall'Oglio, Paolo, 138
Damascus, 5, 93, 173, 201. *See also*
    specific topics
  Ahmad Zahra in, 191–95
  Assad family living in, 102
  chemical attacks in, 175–76
  David in, 2–4, 71–72, 113, 115, 124,
    129, 131f, 131–32, 139–47, 150,
    154, 162, 171–73, 174f, 200, 220,
    225, 240–41, 243
  photographs, 152f, 194f
    downtown Damascus, 123f, 214f
  souk in, 194, 194f
Daraa, Syria, 161–62, 182, 216
Dignity of Syria Initiative, 187–88
Diplomat, The (TV series), 233–34
Dodgers. *See* Los Angeles Dodgers
Dodgertown (Vero Beach, Florida),
    8f, 9, 10, 30
Dowlatshahi, Sherry, 230
Dunlap, Judy (David's 2nd wife)
  careers, 147–48
  childhood, 147
  David and, 1, 2, 4, 147, 149–50, 155,
    171, 206, 222

  marriage, 155f, 155–56
  in David's class, 208
  family background, 147
  in Paris, 155–56, 156f
  photographs, 7f, 155f–57f, 172f,
    209f
  in Syria, 1, 7f, 151, 154–55

Edgewood Arsenal, 12, 13
Egypt, 45
  David in, 48–49, 72
  Egypt-Israel peace treaty, 25, 45, 204
Engel, Eliot, 122
Erdoğan, Recep Tayyip, 221, 225f
Ewald, Mary, 65–66
Ewald, Tom, 63–66, 77, 206
Ewald, William, Jr., 63

Falle, Samuel "Sam," 84–85, 156, 157
Feltman, Jeffrey
  background, 178–79
  on David, 179, 183, 190
  David and, 178–79, 189f
  on Middle East, 188–90
Fidan, Hakan, 219
Fisher, Roger, 136, 137
France-Syria relations, 70, 92–93
Freedman, Robert O., 43–46, 85
Friedman, Thomas, 236

Garza, Alberto, 232–33
Gause, F. Gregory, III, 195–96, 203–4,
    243
Gaza humanitarian crisis
    (2023–present), 190–91
Gaza war, 25, 45, 184f, 185–86
  David and, 185, 230, 236
  hostages, 185–86, 203

reactions to, 186, 190–91, 203, 230, 236

United States and, 203

Gemayel, Bachir, 46

George H. W. Bush Presidential Library and Museum, 95

Ghost Robotics, 209

Ghouta chemical attack, 176

Golan Heights, 139, 140, 204

Gomez, Leo, 233f

Goodgame, Dan, 241

Goodwin, Doris Kearns, 206–7

Graff, Garrett M., 243–44

Griffiths, Martin, 172–74, 174f

Hajjar, Bassam, 173

Hama massacre (1982), 103, 169

Hamas, 121, 185, 203, 236. See also Gaza war

Hariri, Rafic, assassination of, 128–29, 220–21

Harvard Law School's Program on Negotiation (PON), 4, 135

Harvard University, 52–53, 62–64

Center for Middle Eastern Studies, 50, 61, 195, 239–40. See also Safran, Nadav: CIA funding

closed conference on Islam and Muslim politics, 59–61

David at, 3, 4, 49–52, 61–64, 85, 195

Nadav Safran and, 50–52, 57, 59, 61

William Ury and, 135–37

Harvard-NUPI-Trinity Syria Research Project (HNT), 165–67, 171–74

Hay'at Tahrir al-Sham (HTS), 215–17

Herring, Joanne King, 132–33

Hezbollah, 121, 129, 178, 204, 221

Hicks, Donna, 187, 190

Hill, Justin, 231, 232

Holman Stadium/Dodgertown, 8f

Hong, Hye, 209

Huntington, Samuel, 52–53

Husayn ibn Ali, 99

Hussein, Saddam, 41, 64–66, 65f

Iran, 203–4

Donald Trump and, 238

Iranian immigration to Syria, 71, 74–75

Iranian Revolution, 24–25, 40, 41, 103

Iranian Revolutionary Guards, 178

Iran-Iraq War, 39–41, 64, 71, 204

Iran-Syria relations, 71, 180, 203–5, 221, 242–43. See also Assad, Bashar al-: Iran and; Iran-Iraq War

Iraq. See also Hussein, Saddam; Iran-Iraq War

Abu Kamal raid (2008), 150–51

Iraq War, 130, 150, 174

Iraqi invasion of Kuwait, 64–65, 77

Iraqi refugee camps, 159, 178

Islamic State of Iraq and the Levant (ISIL/ISIS), 2, 178, 242

Israel. See also Arab-Israeli conflict

Bashar al-Assad and, 121, 234

David and, 234–35

Donald Trump and, 238–39

David's writings on, 92, 230–31

Operation Wooden Leg, 60–61

Oslo Accords, 83–84

siege of Beirut, 45–46

Israel-Syria relations, 204, 234–35, 243

Israel–United Arab Emirates normalization agreement, 202

262 INDEX

Israel–United Arab Emirates relations, 202–3
Israeli-Palestinian conflict, 25, 45, 104, 140–41, 239
Izaguirre, Ulrico "Rico," 93–94, 96–97, 100, 233f

Jabhat al-Nusra (Al-Nusra Front), 167–69
Jewish exodus from Eastern Europe (1991), 80
John Carroll School, 14–16, 18
Johnny's (Baltimore baseball team), 18–20
Joint Comprehensive Plan of Action (JCPOA), 238
Jolani, Abu Mohammad al- (Ahmed al-Sharaa), 215–17, 225f, 225–26
Jolie, Angelina, 158f, 178
Jones, Jan Laverty, 97

Kayser, Tom, 207–8
Keohane, Robert, 52
Khaddam, Abdul Halim, 118–19, 129
Khan Shaykhun chemical attack, 181
Khomeini, Ayatollah Ruhollah, 24, 40, 41
Kim, Yonghun, 209, 228f, 230, 233f
Kingston, Paul, 69–70
Korean Air Lines Flight 007, 44
Koufax, Sandy, 4, 33
Kuftaro, Ahmed (Grand Mufti of Syria), 138, 140, 142–43
Kuwait, 64, 77
  Iraqi invasion of, 64–65, 77

Lasorda, Tommy, 9, 30
Latakia, 73

David in, 73–74, 222
protests (1999), 107
Latimore, Carey, 211–12
Lebanese Civil War, 46
Lebanon
  David and, 173, 174, 176–77
  Hrair Balian and, 149, 176–77, 190, 191
  Lebanon-Syria border, 173, 177
  Lebanon-Syria relations, 46, 53, 119, 122, 177, 220
  Lebanon War (1982), 45–46
  Lebanon War (2006), 129
  PLO in, 42, 45–46, 60
  Syrian occupation of, 122, 129
  US embassy bombing in Beirut (1983), 47, 47f
Lee, Oliver, 233
Lesch, David W. *See also specific topics*
  awards and honors, 66–67, 156–57, 212f, 213
  blacklisted, 143–44
  characterizations of, 179, 183, 190, 208–9, 213, 230, 233–34, 243–44
  education, 14–19, 26, 34–35
    college, 21, 49. *See also* Central Arizona College; Harvard University; University of Maryland
  employment, 47, 82, 156–57
  finances, 34–35, 47, 82, 156
  grandmother, 192
  injuries, 27
    sports injuries, 31–32, 34, 104, 118
  interrogated, 144, 145
  interviews conducted by, 71, 77, 116–21, 117f, 125, 166–71, 176, 178, 215, 217, 222

interviews of, 79, 205f, 205–6

personal life, 15–16, 18, 32. *See also*
    Dunlap, Judy; Lesch, Suzanne;
    Schaefert, Lisa

philosophy, 127–28, 179, 190, 213,
    234–36, 244

photographs, 7f, 20f, 51f, 98f, 99f,
    130f–31f, 156f, 157f, 172f, 181f,
    189f, 198f, 209f, 228f, 244f

poisoned, 2, 142–43

residences, 51, 55, 62, 68, 76, 104.
    See also Bel Air

sports and, 37, 83

  baseball, 7, 9–10, 14, 17–21, 20f,
      24, 26–29, 44, 49–50, 230,
      244f. *See also* Los Angeles
      Dodgers; Milwaukee Brewers

  basketball, 14, 15, 17, 50, 195

as teacher, 63–64, 131, 146, 156–57,
    208–9, 213

writings, 16, 82, 132, 160, 238

  The Arab-Israeli Conflict: A History,
      147

  "Assad Has Won in Syria. But
      Syria Hardly Exists.," 182

  dissertation, 4–5, 61, 62, 69, 76,
      82, 93, 138

  *A History of the Middle East Since
      the Rise of Islam*, 40, 41, 92,
      237

  "Iran Is Taking Over Syria. Can
      Anyone Stop It?," 204

  *The Middle East and the United
      States: A Historical and Politi-
      cal Reassessment*, 85

  *The New Lion of Damascus: Bashar
      al-Asad and Modern Syria*, 3,
      62, 124, 142, 237

"The Reformer" (screenplay), 193

"The Road to Damascus: The Arabs
    March Back to Befriend
    Assad," 197

*Syria: The Fall of the House of
    Assad*, 108, 122, 160, 240

*Syria and the United States: Eisen-
    hower's Cold War in the Middle
    East*, 69, 82, 116

"The Syrian President I Know," 162

Lesch, Margaret ("Marge") Marie
    Corres (David's mother), 54, 55,
    57, 77, 105, 106

  burn injury from gas explosion/
      house fire, 54–57, 56f

  David and, 13, 37, 54, 55, 106, 155,
      180

  death, 180

  family background, 11–12

  marriage, 12

  Michael Lesch and, 77, 105, 180

  overview, 10, 11

  photograph, 36f

Lesch, Michael (David's son), 105, 106

  birth, 77

  childhood, 104–6, 105f, 111, 127

  David and, 2–4, 111, 127, 150, 151,
      152f, 154–56

  photographs, 7f, 105f, 152f

  relationship with grandmother, 77,
      105, 180

  "Samir" and, 154

  in Syria, 150, 151, 152f, 154

Lesch, Robert "Bob" (David's brother)

  career, 37, 44

  childhood, 10–11, 14

  David and, 10–11, 14, 23, 37, 52,
      55–56, 77, 104

Lesch, Michael *(continued)*
  and his parents, 36f, 54–57, 180
  in Phoenix, 23
  residences, 55, 57
  sports and, 10–11, 14, 37, 44, 104
Lesch, Suzanne (Blais) (David's 1st
    wife), 81, 104, 105
  employment, 48, 62, 68, 77, 81
  relationship with David, 48, 51–52,
    55, 61, 68, 137
  travels, 62, 70
Lesch, Warren (David's father),
    105–6
  burn injury from gas explosion/
    house fire, 54–57, 56f
  career, 11–14
  David and, 106
  death, 106
  education, 11, 12
  marriage to Marge, 11–12
  Michael Lesch (grandson) and, 77,
    105
  photograph, 36f
  sports and, 10, 29–30, 106
London
  Bashar al-Assad in, 99, 103, 116,
    120–21
  David in, 68–72, 240–41
Los Angeles Dodgers, 8f, 9
  David drafted to, 4, 9, 29–30, 30f,
    104, 207–8
  David in, 30–35, 56
  financial support to David, 30,
    34–35, 49
Lynne, Jeff, 120

Maaloula, Syria, 5–6, 134f, 149
Madrid Conference of 1991 (Madrid
    Peace Conference), 80

Major, John, 98f
Maloney, Tim, 231
Maryland
  colleges in, 19, 38. *See also* Univer-
    sity of Maryland
  David in, 76–78. *See also* Bel Air;
    University of Maryland
McCusker, John, 79–83, 98f
McHugh, Gerry, 174–75, 187, 189f,
    223, 243
"Middle East and the United States:
    An Historical Inquiry, The"
    (international conference),
    83–87, 94
Middle East oil production, 24,
    41–42, 89, 90, 92
  oil crisis (1973), 24
Mike's Auto Mart team, 18
Milwaukee Brewers, 20, 21, 28, 32, 42,
    207–8
Ministry of Foreign Affairs and
    Expatriates (Syria), 201, 209
Montaine, Jackie, 211
Mount Qasioun, 124, 125, 152f, 173
Moustapha, Imad, 113, 143, 234
Muhammad, Prophet, 6

Najib, Atef (Bashar al-Assad's
    cousin), 162, 168
National Archives, 67f, 68–70
Netanyahu, Benjamin, 234–35
9/11 terrorist attacks, 110f
  aftermath, 13, 109–12
  David and, 111–12
  description of, 109–11
Nirenberg, Ron, 210–11, 228f, 229–31,
    233
Nome, Frida, 165, 172, 173, 174f
Nye, Joseph, 52

INDEX 265

October 7 attacks, 185. *See also* Gaza war
Operation Wooden Leg, 60–61
Orioles. *See* Baltimore Orioles
Oslo Accords, 83–84
Otaiba, Yousef Al, 202–3

Pahlavi, Mohammad Reza (Shah of Iran), 24, 40, 41
Palestine Liberation Organization (PLO), 42, 46, 47, 60. *See also* Israeli-Palestinian conflict
  in Lebanon, 42, 45–46, 60
Palmyra (Tadmur), 2, 5, 92f, 153
Paris
  Bashar and Asma al-Assad in, 159
  David in, 70–72, 155–56, 156f, 159, 171
  Judy Dunlap in, 155–56, 156f
Pearlman, Wendy, 170–71
Pedersen, Geir, 165, 166, 185–88, 191, 218
Peres, Shimon, 60
Phoenix, David in, 21, 23, 27
Pioneer Baseball League, 31
Price, G. Jefferson, III, 45–46
Public Records Office, 67f, 68–69

Quandt, William, 25

Rabin, Yitzak, 60, 83–84
Reagan, Ronald, 42, 229
Reitz, Doug, 14, 54
Reza Pahlavi, Mohammad (Shah of Iran), 24, 40, 41
Richardson, Kenny, 26–28, 30, 32–33
Riedel, Bruce, 77
Rifai, Samir, 239–40

Ripken, Cal, Sr., 29–30
Rosen, Nir, 167
Rowda Building, Bashar al-Assad's office in, 115, 118, 119, 140
Russia, 44, 80
  Assad family and, 222
  Syria and, 180, 203, 204, 216

Sabra and Shatila massacre, 46
Safran, Nadav
  background, 50–51
  CIA funding, 58f, 59, 61, 62
  closed conference coordinated by, 59–61
  David and, 51, 52, 57, 59, 62
  Harvard University and, 50–52, 57, 59, 61
  photographs, 51f, 58f
  as professor, 50–51, 62
Saghir, George, 165, 167, 168
Salhani, Justin, 46
Salinas, Manolo Jiménez, 210f
"Samir" (Syrian businessman), 141, 145–46, 153, 154
San Antonio, Texas, 82, 84, 230–31. *See also* Trinity University
  David in, 12, 80–81, 87, 94, 104, 130, 175, 198, 210, 212, 228f, 229–32. *See also specific topics*
San Antonio River Walk, 90
Saraperos de Saltillo, 209, 210, 244f
Satloff, Robert "Rob," 51f, 69
Schaefert, Lisa, 18–19, 21, 35, 48
Seale, Patrick, 62, 101, 109
Sepulveda, Juan, 233
Shaaban, Bouthaina, 142, 162, 172, 173, 174f
Shah of Iran (Mohammad Reza Pahlavi), 24, 40, 41

Sharaa, Ahmed al- (Abu Mohammad al-Jolani), 215–17, 225f, 225–26
Shaykhs (basketball team), 50, 51f
Shia Islam/Shiites, 71, 99. *See also* Alawites
Sonoran Desert, Arizona, 22f
South Korea, 209, 230
Southern Syria offensive (2024), 215–21
Soviet Union and Syria, 75, 101
St. John's College, 38
St. Mary's College of Maryland, 77–78
Star Trek, 16–17
Stein, Ansel, 90, 91, 97–98, 100–101
Stoessinger, John, 79
Stryker, Kevin, 197, 208–9, 213
Sufi dancer, x
Summer in Syria program, 98, 99f, 197
Sutor, Dave, 19
Syria. *See also specific topics*
  David's lessons for, 233–34
  David's writings on, 4–5. *See also* Lesch, David: writings
  history, 5–6, 93, 121
  overview, 5–6
  terrorism and, 121–23
Syrian Arab Army, 220, 239
Syrian civil war. *See* Syrian revolution and civil war
Syrian Democratic Forces, 186–87, 218, 241–42
Syrian Desert, 124, 153–54. *See also* Arabian Desert; Palmyra
Syrian prisons, opening of, 218, 218f, 220, 241, 242
Syrian refugee camps, 158f, 159, 178

Syrian revolution and civil war, 161–62, 165, 168–71, 174, 177, 194, 217, 218. *See also* Assad regime
  aftermath, 191, 222–23, 242
  Bashar al-Assad and, 162, 173, 193, 197, 204, 241
  Captagon (fenethylline) and, 239. *See also* Ba'athist Syrian Captagon industry
  casualties, 1, 180
  characterization of, 196–97
  Daraa and, 161–62, 182, 216
  David and, 93, 175, 187, 197, 204, 240, 241
  and the economy, 226
  Harvard-NUPI-Trinity Syria Research Project (HNT), 165–67, 171–74
  Hezbollah and, 204, 221
  human rights violations and war crimes, 162–63, 169–70, 175–76, 182, 241–42
    chemical attacks, 175, 176, 181
  humanitarian impact, 163, 178, 180–82, 186, 226
  Iran and, 204, 216, 221
  Jeffrey Feltman and, 178
  refugees, 178, 180–81, 221, 242
  sanctions against Syria, 165, 226–27
  Syrian Democratic Forces and, 186–87, 218, 241–42
  Syrian opposition, 166–69, 171, 173, 175, 176, 177f, 191, 197, 215–17, 221
  Syrian opposition offensives (2024), 215–17

INDEX

United States and, 165, 168, 178,
186–87, 197
Syrian villa party, Lesch family with
hosts at, 153f
Syria–United States relations, 121–23,
130–32, 177. *See also under* Syrian
revolution and civil war

Tartus, Syria, 72f, 72–73
Temple of Baal, Palmyra, Syria,
92f
Tice, Austin, 200, 202, 203, 220
abduction, 163–64
search for, 183, 197–203, 220
Tice, Debra (Austin's mother)
David and, 164, 175, 198f, 198–
200
Donald Trump and, 200–201
search for Austin, 164, 197–98,
200–203
Tice, Marc (Austin's father), 164, 175,
197, 198f, 199, 201
Tlass, Manaf, 142
Trinity University, 81f, 210–13
David at, 78, 80, 82–83, 86f, 95, 207,
212f, 213
George Bush Institute for Middle
East Studies, 95
history, 78–79
history department, 83
overview, 78
Ron Calgaard at, 79–80, 86f
Trump, Donald
David and, 200, 201, 238–39
election of (2024), 237–39
Iran and, 238
Israel and, 238–39
Syria and, 200, 201, 225–27

and the Tices, 200–201
Tunisia, 60
Turkey, 74–76, 167, 192

Umayyad Mosque, Damascus, 112f
United Arab Emirates (UAE), 202–3,
209
United Nations (UN), 104, 176
David and, 179, 181f, 183
Jeffrey Feltman and, 178, 179
United States. *See also specific topics*
Bashar al-Assad and, 221
Gaza war and, 203
Hafez al-Assad and, 75, 94
State Department, 200–201
Syrian revolution and civil war
and, 165, 168, 178, 186–87, 197.
See also Syria–United States
relations
US embassy bombing in Beirut
(1983), 47, 47f
University of Maryland, Baltimore
County (UMBC), 37–49, 76
Ury, William, 135, 136, 187, 188
Abraham Path Initiative (API) and,
137–39, 141, 143, 149
David and, 135–39, 141–43, 149
dealing with conflict, 137
family background and early life,
136–37
Harvard University and, 135–37
Jimmy Carter and, 136, 149
terms coined by, 206, 236
writings, 137, 188
Uzman, Jacob, 167, 171

Vero Beach, Florida, 30–31. *See also*
Dodgertown

Weiss, John, 135
Wells, Colin, 79
West Bank, 45
Western Maryland College, 19
Whiting fellowship, 66, 68, 71
Wilson, Charlie, 133

Yacoubian, Mona, 179
Y2K (year 2000 problem), 107

Zahra, Ahmad, 191–95

**Catherine Nixon Cooke** is the award-winning author of seven biographies, including *Juan O'Gorman: A Confluence of Civilizations*, *The Thistle and the Rose: Railroads, Romance, and Big Oil in Revolutionary Mexico*, and *In Search of Tom Slick: Explorer and Visionary*, which was produced as the podcast *Tom Slick: Mystery Hunter* in 2024. She is the former CEO of the Mountain Institute, the World Affairs Council of San Antonio, and the Mind Science Foundation. A fellow and medalist of the Explorers Club, she lives on a farm in the Texas Hill Country.

www.ingramcontent.com/pod-product-compliance
Lightning Source LLC
Jackson TN
JSHW070805280725
88001JS00001B/1/J